Daily Skill Builders:
Vocabulary
Grades 4–5

By
CINDY BARDEN

COPYRIGHT © 2007 Mark Twain Media, Inc.

ISBN 978-1-58037-409-5

Printing No. CD-404068

Mark Twain Media, Inc., Publishers
Distributed by Carson-Dellosa Publishing Company, Inc.

Table of Contents

Table of Contents (cont.)

Introduction to the Teacher

Books in the *Daily Skill Builders: Vocabulary* series are designed to increase students' reading, writing, and speaking vocabulary by introducing new words and providing opportunities to determine their meanings and use the words in context. In addition, practice in standardized test-taking is emphasized.

Suggestions for Use

Each activity page is divided into two reproducible sections that can be cut apart and used separately. Activities could be used in class as a group or individually, or they can be assigned as homework. Transparencies of the activities can be made to help students participate as they follow along in class. Extra copies can be kept in your learning center for additional practice.

An alphabetical list of the vocabulary words introduced in this book is included on pages v–vi. Vocabulary words can be included in your weekly spelling list. Use the new words in context in class and encourage students to do so also. Being exposed to and using new words helps students develop a more extensive reading, writing, and speaking vocabulary.

Organization

Vocabulary words are introduced in groups of 10 to 12 words at a time. Four activities are included for each new group of words.

The first activity involves defining the new words. Before students begin this activity, encourage them to read the words out loud together. At this age, many students have difficulty understanding the pronunciation guide in a dictionary. Saying the words helps them learn pronunciation. Students will need access to a good dictionary and a thesaurus. Include both a simple picture dictionary as well as one that is more advanced.

The second and third activities for each group of words offer variety to provide students with many different ways to approach learning vocabulary. They use words in context, write rhyming words and short poems, express opinions, and write sentences. Students learn synonyms and antonyms for words, differentiate between homophones, explore multiple meanings for the same word, write present and past tenses of verbs, use the singular and plural forms of nouns, and change adjectives to adverbs.

Since standardized testing is an important component of education, the fourth activity for each group of words provides practice in standardized test-taking formats. This helps students become familiar and comfortable with the format and provides test-taking practice.

The table of contents identifies the skills that students use to complete each activity. Review pages are included to reinforce what students learned. An answer key is provided at the end of the book.

Both the No Child Left Behind Act and standardized testing require students to meet certain proficiency standards. The *Daily Skill Builders* in this book have been written with both of these sets of requirements in mind. Standards matrixes for selected states are provided on pages vii–ix. These give teachers the specific reading, writing, and language standards that are covered by each activity in this book. The National ELA Standards as supported by NCTE and IRA are listed on page x.

Vocabulary Words Used in This Book

absolute
absolutely
accelerate
accomplish
accomplishment
actual
actually
adequate
adequately
adjust
adjustment
advance
advancement
advertise
advertisement
agree
ambulance
amend
amendment
amplify
annual
annually
anxious
anxiously
apology
appropriate
aqueduct
ascend
assemble
assign
assignment
assume
attempt
attract
attraction
audience
auditorium
automobile
available
aviation
awkward
bachelor

backspace
backup
bay
bayou
belief
believable
biologist
biology
blizzard
borrow
botanist
botany
boundary
brainstorm
bullheaded
butterfingers
canyon
capable
cargo
carnival
carriage
catalog
cavern
champion
chemist
chemistry
circular
climate
cloudburst
collapse
collect
collection
coma
combination
combine
comma
committee
companion
compare
comparison
compass
compassion

compete
competition
complain
concentrate
concentration
conclude
conclusion
conflict
consider
consideration
construct
construction
continent
continue
contribute
contribution
convene
convention
convince
cottonmouth
coward
crop
crossover
crowbar
custodian
customer
daybreak
decrease
defend
delay
delegate
delegation
delicious
delivery
demonstrate
demonstration
denial
deny
depart
deposit
deputy
descend

desert
desirable
despise
dessert
detain
detention
diagonal
disagree
disbelief
discontinue
discovery
dishonest
dog paddle
dogtrot
drastic
drastically
duty
embarrass
embarrassment
employ
employment
equality
equator
equip
equipment
erase
erosion
essential
exact
exactly
examination
examine
excite
excitement
exhale
experience
explain
explanation
export
exterior
external
fabric

factory
factual
fatigue
fictional
field
finish
firsthand
flexible
floodlights
footloose
forecast
former
formerly
foundation
fragrance
frequent
frigid
frigidly
fumble
garment
gather
gaze
generous
geologist
geology
gigantic
glacier
gorgeous
gradual
gradually
grasp
groundskeeper
halfway
hardship
hardware
headfirst
headlight
headline
headway
hedgehog
helicopter
hemisphere

Vocabulary Words Used in This Book (cont.)

high-handed	kneecap	opportunity	rapidly	supervisor
historian	known	overcome	rattlesnake	sympathy
honest	latitude	overdo	recognize	symphony
horseplay	layover	overdue	refrigerate	talent
horseradish	legislate	overshoes	refrigeration	technology
humidity	legislature	overturn	regular	telescope
hurricane	limited	overview	regularly	temporary
ignorance	liter	panic	relative	tenant
ignore	litter	parachute	reply	tenderhearted
immediate	litterbug	payday	represent	tightfisted
immediately	livestock	pebble	representative	tight-lipped
import	loan	peek	rescue	tornado
impossible	locate	penalty	roadrunner	tradition
impractical	location	peninsula	roam	turnover
improper	longitude	permanent	rollover	turtledove
improve	lunar	pigeonhole	sailfish	typical
improvement	manage	plantation	sapsucker	typically
inappropriate	management	platform	sawhorse	unavailable
incapable	marine	polecat	scientist	unbelievable
increase	mathematician	possible	scold	underdog
individual	maximum	practical	screwdriver	underfoot
inequality	meadow	precipitation	secondary	understudy
infect	melody	prejudice	seldom	undesirable
infection	memory	prescription	severe	underhanded
inflexible	merchant	pretend	shiver	unknown
inform	minimum	prevent	silkworm	unlimited
information	mischief	prevention	silverfish	unnecessary
ingredient	moderate	previous	sincere	usual
inhale	moderately	previously	situate	usually
insincere	modify	primary	situation	variety
instant	moisture	produce	sketch	vehicle
instantly	monkeyshines	production	sleet	victory
instruct	motorcycle	proper	slender	visual
instruction	museum	property	snapdragon	visually
interest	natural	protect	solar	volcano
interior	naturally	protection	sourpuss	wander
internal	necessary	protest	stagecoach	wetsuit
irrigate	nightmare	provide	stall	wolfhound
irritate	obvious	provisions	stellar	wonder
isthmus	obviously	purchase	stockroom	zephyr
jellyfish	occupy	pushover	stockyard	zoologist
keen	offer	quantity	structure	zoology
keenly	office	rapid	summarize	

California Standards Matrix for Grades 4–5

LANGUAGE ARTS STANDARDS	ACTIVITIES
READING	
Use word origins, synonyms, antonyms, homophones, homographs, and idioms to determine the meaning of words.	4, 5, 6, 7, 8, 10, 12, 14, 16, 17, 20, 21,22, 24, 25, 28, 33, 35, 36, 40, 42, 44, 45, 48, 51, 52, 53, 57, 58, 60, 61, 62, 64, 66, 67, 68, 72, 76, 77, 78, 80, 81, 84, 85, 88, 92, 96, 97, 99, 100, 104, 105, 106, 107, 108, 109, 111, 114, 118, 121, 122, 124, 125, 126, 129, 130, 133, 134, 135, 142, 144, 146, 148, 150, 154, 156, 158, 162
Know abstracts, derived roots, and affixes from Greek and Latin and use this knowledge to analyze the meaning of complex words (e.g., controversial).	37, 38, 41, 43, 46, 49, 54, 56, 65, 69, 71, 73, 74, 75, 83, 89, 119, 127, 129, 145, 151, 152, 153, 159
Use a dictionary and thesaurus to determine meaning and other features of unknown words.	1, 5, 9, 13, 17, 21, 23, 29, 37, 41, 43, 45, 46, 49, 50, 57, 61, 65, 73, 77, 85, 89, 93,101, 111, 115, 119, 124, 127, 128, 129, 132, 139, 140, 143, 145, 147, 152, 155, 159
Make, modify, and confirm inferences, conclusions, or generalizations about text and support them with textual evidence and prior knowledge.	14, 18, 26, 30, 31, 47, 66, 93, 94, 102, 120, 128
Distinguish between cause and effect and between fact and opinion in expository text.	63, 79, 95, 113, 157
WRITING	
Create well-developed, multiple-paragraph narrative and expository compositions.	15, 39, 59, 91, 94, 117
Use traditional structures for conveying information (e.g., similarity/ differences, cause/effect).	63, 94, 103
Use organizational features of printed text to locate relevant information.	82, 93, 94, 103
Create simple documents by using electronic media and employing organizational features (e.g., passwords, entry and pull-down menus, word searches, a thesaurus, spell checks).	149
Write personal and formal letters, thank-you notes, and invitations.	149
Write narratives that establish a plot, point of view, setting, and conflict.	59, 75 ,117
Write research reports that frame questions for investigation, establish a controlling idea, and develop the topic with simple facts, details, examples, and explanations.	94
LANGUAGE CONVENTIONS	
Identify and use regular and irregular verbs, adverbs, prepositions, and coordinating conjunctions.	9, 11, 41, 43, 49, 50, 54, 55, 59, 89, 90, 91, 115, 116, 117, 138, 145, 147, 149 ,152
Identify and correctly use verbs that are often misused (e.g., lie / lay), modifiers, and pronouns.	2, 155, 156
Spell roots, affixes, contractions, and syllable constructions correctly.	27, 43, 46, 47, 59, 70, 73, 117, 131, 132

Florida Standards Matrix for Grades 4–5

LANGUAGE ARTS STANDARDS	ACTIVITIES
READING	
Use a variety of strategies to determine meaning and increase vocabulary (e.g., affixes, multiple-meaning words, antonyms, synonyms, root words, homonyms, homophones).	4, 5, 6, 8, 12, 16, 20, 22, 24, 25, 28, 31, 33, 35, 36, 37, 40, 41, 42, 43, 45, 46, 47, 48, 49, 51, 52, 53, 56, 57, 58, 60, 62, 64, 65, 67, 68, 69, 70, 71, 72, 73, 74, 75, 76, 77, 80, 81, 83, 84, 85, 88, 90, 92, 96, 97, 100, 102, 104, 105, 106, 108, 109, 114, 118, 119, 121, 122, 124, 125, 126, 127, 128, 129, 130, 135, 142, 143, 144, 146, 148, 150, 151, 152, 154, 155, 156 ,158, 159, 162
Use resources, such as dictionary, thesaurus, and context, to build word meanings.	1, 5, 7, 9, 10, 13, 14, 17, 21, 22, 23, 29, 30, 37, 41, 44, 45, 49, 61, 65, 73, 77, 85, 89, 93, 99, 101, 107, 111, 115, 119, 124, 128, 132, 139, 140, 143, 145, 147, 153, 155, 159
Understand explicit and implicit ideas and information in texts (e.g., main idea, inferences, fact vs. opinion, order of events).	79, 95, 113
Read and organize information from multiple sources for a variety of purposes (e.g., to support opinions, predictions, and conclusions; to write a research report; to conduct interviews).	14, 18, 30, 82, 93, 94
Understand a variety of textual organizations (e.g., comparison/contrast, cause/effect, sequence of events).	103, 113
WRITING	
Establish a purpose for writing (e.g., explaining, informing, entertaining, making a request).	3, 6, 14, 15, 18, 19, 23, 26, 31, 59, 94, 117, 131, 149
Use an effective organizational pattern and substantial support to achieve completeness.	15, 59, 94, 103, 117
Use devices to develop relationships among ideas (e.g., transitional devices; paragraphs that show a change in time, idea, or place; cause-and-effect relationships).	63, 94, 103, 113
Use a variety of sentence structures to reinforce ideas.	15, 39, 59, 91, 94, 103, 117, 149
Use conventions of punctuation and capitalization.	15, 23, 39, 59, 87, 91, 94, 103, 117, 136, 142, 149, 152, 161
Use a variety of spelling strategies.	15, 39, 59, 87, 91, 94, 103, 117, 152
Use various parts of speech correctly in writing (e.g., subject-verb agreement, noun and verb forms, objective and subjective case pronouns, correct form of adjectives and adverbs).	2, 9, 11, 15, 23, 39, 42, 47, 50, 51, 54, 55, 59, 62, 71, 73, 74, 75, 78, 83, 85, 86, 87, 89, 90, 91, 94, 103, 111, 112, 115, 116, 117, 131, 133, 134, 136, 138, 141, 145, 149, 152, 156, 161
Use basic features of page format, including paragraph indentations and margins.	15, 39, 59, 91, 94, 103, 117, 149
Write for a variety of occasions, audiences, and purposes (e.g., letters to invite or thank, stories or poems to entertain, information to record, notes and observations reflecting comprehension).	14, 15, 18, 23, 26, 27, 30, 31, 34, 38, 39, 47, 50, 51, 59, 66, 69, 75, 82, 87, 91, 94, 103, 117, 120, 128, 131, 133, 136, 141, 145, 149, 152, 160, 161
LANGUAGE	
Use appropriate words (e.g., connotative and idiomatic meanings, figurative language, sensory words) to shape reactions, perceptions, and beliefs.	39, 59, 75, 91, 117
Vary language (e.g., appropriate tone, content, vocabulary) according to situation, audience, and purpose.	15, 39, 59, 75, 91, 94, 117
Understand symbols, similes, metaphors, analogies, alliteration, and idiomatic language.	161

Texas Standards Matrix for Grades 4–5

LANGUAGE ARTS STANDARDS	ACTIVITIES
READING	
Apply knowledge of letter-sound correspondences, language structure, and context to recognize words.	1, 2, 4, 5, 7, 8, 10, 12, 14, 16, 18, 20, 22, 24, 25, 28, 30, 31, 33, 35, 36, 37, 40, 42, 44, 45, 47, 48, 49, 51, 52, 53 ,58, 60, 62, 64, 65, 67, 68, 69, 71, 72, 73, 74, 76, 77, 78, 81, 84, 85, 88, 92, 96, 97, 99, 100, 104, 105, 106, 107, 108, 109, 114, 118, 119, 121, 122, 124, 125, 126, 127, 128, 129, 130, 132, 134, 135, 142, 143, 144, 145, 146, 148, 150, 153, 154, 155, 156, 158, 159, 162
Use structural analysis to identify root words with affixes.	11, 41, 43, 46, 49, 56, 65, 69, 73, 74, 75, 83, 89, 119, 127, 151, 152
Locate the meanings, pronunciations, and derivations of unfamiliar words using a dictionary, a thesaurus, a glossary, and available technology.	1, 5, 9, 13, 17, 21, 23, 29, 37, 41, 43, 45, 49, 65, 73, 77, 85, 89, 93, 101, 111, 15, 119, 124, 132, 139, 140, 143, 145, 147, 155, 159
Draw on experiences to bring meanings to words in context, such as interpreting figurative language and multiple-meaning words.	3, 6, 57, 71, 102, 120
Draw and describe mental images that text descriptions evoke.	31, 94, 117
Distinguish fact and opinion in various texts.	79, 95, 157
Answer different types and levels of questions.	8, 14, 20, 44, 68, 76, 90, 126, 130
Represent text information in different ways, such as in outlines, timelines, and graphic organizers.	94
LITERARY RESPONSE AND CONCEPTS	
Offer observations, make connections, react, speculate, interpret, and raise questions in response to texts.	3, 6, 9, 14, 18, 26, 30, 31, 34, 38, 39, 47, 66, 70, 94, 102, 106, 120, 128
Interpret text ideas through journal writing, discussion, enactment, and media.	39, 117
Support responses by referring to relevant aspects of text and own experiences.	14, 18, 31, 34, 38, 39, 47, 94
Form and revise questions for investigations.	94
WRITING	
Write for a variety of audiences and purposes, such as to express, to influence, to inform, to entertain, to record, to problem solve, and to reflect.	3, 6, 15, 18, 19, 23, 26, 27, 30, 31, 34, 38, 39, 46, 47, 50, 51, 59, 63, 66, 75, 82, 87, 91, 94, 103, 113, 117, 131, 133 ,136, 141, 145, 149, 152, 160, 161
Compose original texts, applying the conventions of written language, such as capitalization, punctuation, and penmanship, to communicate clearly.	15, 23, 39, 59, 75, 87, 91, 94, 103, 117, 149
Write with accurate spelling of roots, inflections, affixes, and syllable constructions.	11, 15, 23, 27, 39, 43, 46, 47, 55, 59, 65, 70, 73, 75, 91, 94, 103, 117, 132, 141, 149, 152, 161
Use regular and irregular plurals correctly and adjust verbs for agreement.	17, 23, 59, 91, 94, 103, 117, 132, 134, 149, 152
Write in complete sentences, varying the types, such as compound and complex, to match meanings and purposes.	15, 19, 23, 39, 59, 75, 87, 91, 94, 103, 117, 131, 136, 141, 149, 152, 161
Use adjectives and adverbs appropriately to make writing vivid and precise.	59, 61, 62, 66, 75, 83, 85, 86, 87, 89, 90, 91, 94, 103, 111, 112, 115, 116, 117, 136, 138, 149, 152, 161
Use prepositional phrases and conjunctions to elaborate and connect ideas meaningfully.	59, 75, 91, 94, 103, 117, 149
Use the writing process to develop compositions.	15, 39, 91, 94, 103, 117, 149

National ELA Standards

(as supported by NCTE and IRA)

[reference: http://www.ncte.org/about/over/standards/110846.htm]

1. Students read a wide range of print and nonprint texts to build an understanding of texts, of themselves, and of the cultures of the United States and the world; to acquire new information; to respond to the needs and demands of society and the workplace; and for personal fulfillment. Among these texts are fiction and nonfiction, classic and contemporary works.

2. Students read a wide range of literature from many periods in many genres to build an understanding of the many dimensions (e.g., philosophical, ethical, aesthetic) of human experience.

3. Students apply a wide range of strategies to comprehend, interpret, evaluate, and appreciate texts. They draw on their prior experience, their interactions with other readers and writers, their knowledge of word meaning and of other texts, their word identification strategies, and their understanding of textual features (e.g., sound-letter correspondence, sentence structure, context, graphics).

4. Students adjust their use of spoken, written, and visual language (e.g., conventions, style, vocabulary) to communicate effectively with a variety of audiences and for different purposes.

5. Students employ a wide range of strategies as they write and use different writing process elements appropriately to communicate with different audiences for a variety of purposes.

6. Students apply knowledge of language structure, language conventions (e.g., spelling and punctuation), media techniques, figurative language, and genre to create, critique, and discuss print and nonprint texts.

7. Students conduct research on issues and interests by generating ideas and questions, and by posing problems. They gather, evaluate, and synthesize data from a variety of sources (e.g., print and nonprint texts, artifacts, people) to communicate their discoveries in ways that suit their purpose and audience.

8. Students use a variety of technological and information resources (e.g., libraries, databases, computer networks, video) to gather and synthesize information and to create and communicate knowledge.

9. Students develop an understanding of and respect for diversity in language use, patterns, and dialects across cultures, ethnic groups, geographic regions, and social roles.

10. Students whose first language is not English make use of their first language to develop competency in the English language arts and to develop understanding of content across the curriculum.

11. Students participate as knowledgeable, reflective, creative, and critical members of a variety of literacy communities.

12. Students use spoken, written, and visual language to accomplish their own purposes (e.g., for learning, enjoyment, persuasion, and the exchange of information).

ACTIVITY 5 Match Words That Are Antonyms

Name: _____

Date: _____

Antonyms are words that have opposite meanings. Match the words with their antonyms. Use a dictionary if you are not sure of the meaning of a word.

_____ 1. decrease
_____ 2. exhale
_____ 3. exterior
_____ 4. frequent
_____ 5. permanent
_____ 6. primary
_____ 7. famous
_____ 8. winding
_____ 9. customer
_____ 10. bright

a. temporary
b. unknown
c. straight
d. interior
e. increase
f. seldom
g. seller
h. dreary
i. inhale
j. secondary

ACTIVITY 6 Recognize Antonyms

Name: _____

Date: _____

Antonyms are words that mean the opposite. *Coward* and *hero* are antonyms.

Use the words from the list to write six sets of antonyms.

decrease	exhale	exterior	frequent	increase	inhale
interior	permanent	primary	secondary	seldom	temporary

1. _____ and _____
2. _____ and _____
3. _____ and _____
4. _____ and _____
5. _____ and _____
6. _____ and _____

7. What color is the exterior of your school? _____
8. What color is the interior of your lunchroom? _____
9. What food do you seldom eat for breakfast? _____
10. What snack do you eat frequently? _____

3

ACTIVITY 7 Use Words in Context

Name: _____

Date: _____

Write words from the list to complete the sentences.

decrease	exhale	frequent	inhale	interior
permanent	primary	secondary	seldom	temporary

1. _____ snacking can make you gain weight.
2. When you _____ too much pepper, it makes you sneeze.
3. The pyramids were meant to be a _____ monument to the kings.
4. The cost was of _____ concern to Jamie, who mainly wanted to find the best gift for his parents.
5. As the sun went down, the temperature began to _____.
6. My _____ goal today is to finish this book. Everything else can wait.
7. When you _____, you breathe out carbon dioxide.
8. Ray liked to sleep late. He _____ woke before noon.
9. The _____ of Tom's home is furnished with antiques.
10. The tribe made a _____ camp for the summer.

ACTIVITY 8 Test-Taking

Name: _____

Date: _____

Write the letter of the answer that is the antonym of each word.

_____ 1. decrease   a. increase   b. subtract   c. go down   d. reduce

_____ 2. exhale   a. breathe in   b. breathe out   c. deep breath   d. sigh

_____ 3. exterior   a. outside   b. inside   c. the roof   d. a room

_____ 4. frequent   a. always   b. occasionally   c. often   d. seldom

_____ 5. increase   a. decrease   b. more   c. go up   d. add to

_____ 6. inhale   a. breathe in   b. cough   c. breathe out   d. sneeze

_____ 7. interior   a. furniture   b. warmth   c. outside   d. inside

_____ 8. permanent   a. short-term   b. for a while   c. lasting   d. seldom

_____ 9. primary   a. most important   b. less important   c. first   d. school

_____ 10. secondary   a. most important   b. less important   c. next   d. last

_____ 11. seldom   a. unusual   b. frequent   c. infrequent   d. rarely

_____ 12. temporary   a. short-term   b. permanent   c. seldom   d. cheap

ACTIVITY 13 Define Weather Words

Name: _____

Date: _____

Write the word from the list that best matches the definition. Use a dictionary if you are not sure of the meaning of a word.

> blizzard   climate   forecast   humidity   hurricane
> moisture   precipitation   sleet   tornado   zephyr

1. _____ frozen rain that falls to Earth
2. _____ a funnel-shaped storm with strong whirling winds that comes from a cloud and touches the earth
3. _____ a gentle wind
4. _____ a tropical storm with strong winds that rotate around an eye
5. _____ a very bad snowstorm
6. _____ moisture that falls from clouds
7. _____ the amount of moisture in the air
8. _____ the pattern of weather in an area over a long time
9. _____ to predict
10. _____ all forms of water, including rain and fog

ACTIVITY 14 Expand Knowledge of Weather Words

Name: _____

Date: _____

Use any reference sources to answer the questions.

1. A *blizzard* is a very bad snowstorm. Besides snow, what other conditions would occur during a blizzard? _____

2. *Climate* is the pattern of weather for an area over a long period. What is the difference between *weather* and *climate*? _____

3. *Humidity* is measured in percent. When the humidity is 100% in an area, what type of weather would be most likely? _____

4. A *hurricane* forms over a large body of water, such as an ocean. To be classed as a hurricane, winds must be over how many miles per hour? _____

5. Rain is one form of *precipitation*. What other words are types of precipitation?

   _____

6. *To forecast* means *to predict*. What is the weather forecast for your area tomorrow?

   _____

7. A *tornado* is a funnel-shaped storm cloud that touches down on land. What other types of weather are common during a tornado? _____

8. A *zephyr* is a gentle wind. List other words that mean wind.

   _____

ACTIVITY 15 Use Words in Context/
Write a Weather Report

Name:_____

Date:_____

Write a short weather report. Use at least five of the weather words from the list. Underline all weather words, even those not on the list. Use another sheet of paper if you need more room.

blizzard	climate	humidity	hurricane	moisture
precipitation	forecast	sleet	tornado	zephyr

_____

_____

_____

_____

_____

_____

_____

_____

ACTIVITY 16 Test-Taking

Name:_____

Date:_____

Write the letter of the answer that best matches the definition.

_____ 1. frozen rain that falls to the ground

  a. sleet   b. snow   c. hail   d. moisture

_____ 2. the amount of moisture in the air

  a. rain   b. snow   c. humidity   d. sleet

_____ 3. a large storm that forms over water with winds over 74 miles per hour

  a. tornado   b. hurricane   c. blizzard   d. thunderstorm

_____ 4. water; wetness

  a. lake   b. ocean   c. river   d. moisture

_____ 5. any type of falling moisture, such as rain, snow, sleet, or hail

  a. precipitation b. tornado   c. hurricane   d. forecast

_____ 6. to predict

  a. guess   b. know   c. forecast   d. rain

_____ 7. a bad snowstorm

  a. tornado   b. blizzard   c. hurricane   d. shower

_____ 8. the pattern of weather in an area over a long period of time

  a. climate   b. cold front   c. rain   d. dry and hot

ACTIVITY 17 Define Words That Are Nouns

Name:_____

Date:_____

Nouns are words that name people, places, things, or ideas. All of the words on this list are places. Use a dictionary to write a short definition for each noun.

1. bay _____
2. bayou _____
3. canyon _____
4. continent _____
5. factory _____
6. isthmus _____
7. meadow _____
8. office _____
9. peninsula _____
10. plantation _____

Plural means more than one. Write the plural of each word. Use a dictionary if you are not sure of the correct spelling.

11. factory _____
12. bay _____
13. peninsula _____
14. meadow _____

ACTIVITY 18 Use Reference Sources

Name:_____

Date:_____

Proper nouns name specific people, places, things, or ideas. Use reference sources to find the answers. Capitalize all proper nouns.

1. Name the seven continents. _____ _____ _____
   _____ _____ _____ _____

2. What U.S. state is a large peninsula? _____

3. Green Bay is the name of a city. In what state is it? _____

4. What is the name of the most famous canyon in the United States?
   _____

5. Name a factory in or near your city. _____

6. What do they make at that factory? _____

7. Name someone who works in an office and explain the kind of work that person does.
   _____

8. What might you find growing in a meadow? _____

9. What might you find growing on a plantation? _____

10. What kinds of animals would you likely find in a bayou? _____

ACTIVITY 19 **Write Rhymes**

Name:_____

Date:_____

When writing rhymes for words with one syllable, you can also use words of two or more syllables.   *Example: bay* rhymes with *hooray* and *relay*

When writing rhymes for words with two or more syllables, consider the whole word or only the last syllable of the word.

Examples: *Dalmatian* rhymes with *plantation* in the final syllable. *Candle* and *handle* rhyme in both syllables.

List as many rhymes as you can for each word. Then write a short rhyming sentence for each word on the back of this page.

1. bay _____

   _____

2. bayou _____

   _____

3. plantation _____

   _____

ACTIVITY 20 **Test-Taking**

Name:_____

Date:_____

Circle "T" for true or "F" for false.

1. T F   An **isthmus** is another name for a peninsula.

2. T F   A **continent** is land with water on three sides.

3. T F   People who work in an **office** most likely use telephones and computers.

4. T F   A **meadow** is a place you would likely find alligators.

5. T F   A **bay** is a large body of water with an island.

6. T F   A **canyon** is a deep valley with steep sides.

7. T F   Pineapple and sugar cane are grown on **plantations**.

8. T F   Pickles, cars, candy bars, and bicycles are made in **factories**.

9. T F   You would not be likely to find penguins in a **bayou**.

10. T F   A **peninsula** is a body of water surrounded by land on three sides.

ACTIVITY 21 Define Compound Words

Name:_____

Date:_____

A **compound word** combines two or more words to make a new word that expresses a single idea. *Sunlight, butterfly*, and *whatsoever* are compound words. Sometimes you can learn the meaning of a compound word by looking at the words used.

Draw a line to separate the words used to make the compound word. Write a definition for each compound word. Use a dictionary if you are not sure of the meaning of the word.

1. backspace _____
2. cloudburst _____
3. daybreak _____
4. floodlights _____
5. halfway _____
6. headlight _____
7. kneecap _____
8. screwdriver _____
9. underfoot _____

ACTIVITY 22 Use Compound Words in Context

Name:_____

Date:_____

Write the word from the list that best completes each sentence. Underline all compound words used in the sentences.

cloudburst	daybreak	halfway	headlight
kneecap	payday	screwdriver	underfoot

1. We planned to leave on our daylong fishing trip at _____.

2. Dad had to replace the left _____ on our car before we could get underway.

3. On our way to Greenwood Lake, we stopped for breakfast at the _____ point.

4. If you hand me the _____, I can fix the birdhouse.

5. Kari banged her _____ on the corner of the cupboard in the hallway.

6. My bulldog is always _____ when I try to do housework.

7. Next _____, Callie plans to buy a new armchair for her houseboat.

8. After the _____, the floodwater filled the underpass.

ACTIVITY 23   Write and Use New Compound Words

Name:_____

Date:_____

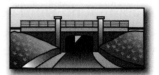

Many compound words begin or end with the words *over* or *under*.
Examples: overdone, overgrown, overlook, and turnover
underdone, underage, and underarm

1. Write 10 or more compound words that include the word *over*. Use a dictionary if you need ideas. _____

_____

2. Write 10 or more compound words that begin with *under*. Use a dictionary if you need ideas.

_____

_____

Write two sentences that use compound words that contain the words *over* or *under*. Use at least two compound words in each sentence.

3. _____

_____

4. _____

_____

ACTIVITY 24   Test-Taking

Name:_____

Date:_____

Circle "T" for true or "F" for false.

1. T   F   A **headlight** is an important part of a car.

2. T   F   A **kneecap** is a cap worn on the knee.

3. T   F   A **screwdriver** is a tool used for driving screws into wood.

4. T   F   **Cloudbursts** occur when an airplane flies through the clouds and breaks them.

5. T   F   **Daybreak** is another word for dawn.

6. T   F   **Floodlights** are lights used after a flood if the power goes out.

7. T   F   If you meet someone **halfway**, you meet in the middle.

8. T   F   **Payday** is the day workers receive their wages.

9. T   F   To **backspace** means to move backwards one space when typing.

10. T   F   When someone is **underfoot**, it means he is in the way.

ACTIVITY 25 Review Nouns and Antonyms

Name:_____

Date:_____

Circle the words on the list that are nouns.

bay	bayou	blizzard	canyon	climate	continent
decrease	exhale	exterior	frequent	gather	hurricane
increase	inhale	interior	meadow	peninsula	permanent
precipitation	primary	secondary	seldom	temporary	zephyr

Use words from the list to write six pairs of antonyms.

1. _____ and _____

2. _____ and _____

3. _____ and _____

4. _____ and _____

5. _____ and _____

6. _____ and _____

ACTIVITY 26 Show Understanding of Review Words by Writing Examples

Name:_____

Date:_____

Give two brief examples for each listing. The first one has been done for you.

1. exterior object ___*a tree and a lake*_____

2. primary needs _____

3. relatives _____

4. supervisors _____

5. precipitation _____

6. something temporary _____

7. forecasts _____

8. peninsulas _____

9. companions _____

10. frequent events _____

11. common nouns _____

12. things you gather _____

13. interior places _____

ACTIVITY 27   Review Compound Words

Name:_____

Date:_____

Combine the words on the list to write 12 or more compound words.

back	ball	break	burst	cap	cloud	day	driver
flood	foot	half	head	knee	over	lights	pads
pay	screw	space	tail	under	way		

_____   _____

_____   _____

_____   _____

_____   _____

_____   _____

_____   _____

_____   _____

ACTIVITY 28   Define Review Words

Name:_____

Date:_____

Match the words with their definitions.

_____ 1. pretend   a. a person who is too afraid to do what must be done

_____ 2. bay   b. to strongly dislike

_____ 3. customer   c. to stare; to look at for a long time

_____ 4. humidity   d. a deep valley with steep sides

_____ 5. assume   e. the amount of moisture in the air

_____ 6. climate   f. to talk into; to persuade

_____ 7. convince   g. a shopper; one who buys things

_____ 8. gaze   h. to protest; to whine

_____ 9. zephyr   i. the pattern of weather in an area over a long time

_____ 10. coward   j. a group of people working towards a goal

_____ 11. canyon   k. moisture that falls from clouds

_____ 12. committee   l. a gentle wind

_____ 13. despise   m. to take for granted; to suppose

_____ 14. precipitation n. to imagine; to make believe

_____ 15. complain   o. an area of water bordered by land on three sides

ACTIVITY 29 Define Words That Are Nouns

Name:_____

Date:_____

Nouns are words that name people, places, things, or ideas. All the nouns on this list name things. Match the words with their definitions. Use a dictionary if you are not sure of the meaning of a word.

_____ 1. carnival

_____ 2. fabric

_____ 3. foundation

_____ 4. garment

_____ 5. ingredients

_____ 6. pebble

_____ 7. platform

_____ 8. prescription

_____ 9. structure

_____ 10. telescope

a. an article of clothing

b. a very small stone

c. a building, for example

d. a celebration; a fair or circus

e. medicine ordered by a doctor

f. a device used to see far out into space

g. a raised stand or stage

h. the base of a building, for example

i. parts used to make something such as cookies

j. cloth

ACTIVITY 30 Apply Vocabulary Words to Everyday Life

Name:_____

Date:_____

Use any type of reference source to answer the questions.

1. A **carnival** can mean any type of celebration. A fair is sometimes called a carnival. A special celebration called Carnivale is held in many large cities on "Fat Tuesday." Fat Tuesday is the day before what religious event that lasts 40 days? _____

2. Wool and cotton are types of **fabrics**. List other fabrics. _____

3. A **foundation** is a sturdy base for a building. List another meaning for *foundation*.

_____

4. A **garment** is an article of clothing made from material. List five garments you might wear.

_____

5. What **ingredients** are needed to make bread? _____

6. **Pebbles** are small stones. When stones are crushed, what are they called?

_____

7. A **platform** could be a stage. Name another type of a platform.

_____

8. **Prescription** medicines are ones ordered by a doctor. What are "over-the-counter" medicines? _____

ACTIVITY 31 Use Critical-Thinking Skills Name:_____

Date:_____

Use your own ideas to write the answers. There are no wrong answers.

1. If you went to a carnival, what would you expect to hear, see, and do? _____
_____

2. What is your favorite fabric? _____

3. What would you most like to look at through a telescope? _____

4. Make up a recipe for something silly. List three or more ingredients needed.
My recipe is for: _____ Ingredients: _____
_____

5. If you had a "magic" pebble, what power would it give you? _____

6. If you could someday stand on the platform as an Olympic winner, what event would you be most likely to win? _____

7. Why do you think some medicines can only be bought if you have a prescription?
_____

8. If you were in a woods without a tent, what could you use to build a structure to spend the night? _____

9. On another sheet of paper, draw or describe a garment a person might wear in outer space.

ACTIVITY 32 Test-Taking Name:_____

Date:_____

Write the letter of the picture that best represents each noun.

A.   B.   C.

D.   E.   F.

G.   H.   I.

1. _____ carnival   2. _____ foundation   3. _____ ingredients
4. _____ platform   5. _____ structure   6. _____ fabric
7. _____ garment   8. _____ pebbles   9. _____ prescription

ACTIVITY 33 Write Synonyms and Antonyms for Verbs

Name: _____

Date: _____

Verbs are action words. All the words on this list are verbs. **Synonyms** are words that mean the same, or nearly the same, as another word. **Antonyms** are words that mean the opposite.

Write a synonym and an antonym for each verb. Use a dictionary if you are not sure of the meaning of a word.

	Synonym	**Antonym**
1. collapse	_____	_____
2. depart	_____	_____
3. erase	_____	_____
4. finish	_____	_____
5. peek	_____	_____
6. reply	_____	_____
7. rescue	_____	_____
8. shiver	_____	_____
9. wander	_____	_____
10. wonder	_____	_____

ACTIVITY 34 Draw on Previous Personal Experience

Name: _____

Date: _____

1. What could cause a building to collapse? _____

2. What do you think of people who are not ready when it is time to depart?

   _____

3. When using a computer, how do you erase a mistake? _____

4. Which is easier for you: to get started on a project or to finish it?

   _____

5. Why do you think little children like to play peek-a-boo? _____

   _____

6. Would you like a job someday that involves rescuing people? _____
   Why or why not? _____

7. Besides cold, what makes you shiver? _____

8. Do you enjoy wandering in the woods? _____ Why or why not?

   _____

9. What is one thing that really makes you wonder? _____

   _____

ACTIVITY 35 Use Words in Context

Name:_____

Date:_____

Write words from the list to complete the sentences.

collapse	depart	erase	finish	peek
reply	rescue	shiver	wander	wonder

1. Does listening to ghost stories make you _____?
2. Grant said, "Don't _____. I have a surprise for you."
3. Wouldn't it be great if we could _____ mistakes in life as easily as we can on a computer?
4. Jill likes to _____ around the mall for hours, even when she doesn't need to buy anything.
5. Ashley was so tired after the race, she was ready to _____.
6. When you receive a letter, it is polite to send a _____.
7. I often _____ if anyone lives on other planets.
8. What time does your plane _____ for Kalamazoo?
9. Corey called the _____ squad to get her cat down from the top of the barn.
10. What time do you expect to _____ your chores?

ACTIVITY 36 Test-Taking

Name:_____

Date:_____

Write "A" if the two words are antonyms. Write "S" if the words are synonyms.

1. _____ wander   roam
2. _____ rescue   save
3. _____ rescue   capture
4. _____ reply   answer
5. _____ depart   leave
6. _____ shiver   still
7. _____ finish   start
8. _____ depart   arrive
9. _____ wander   stay
10. _____ collapse   fall

11. _____ shiver   shake
12. _____ erase   write
13. _____ reply   ask
14. _____ peek   look
15. _____ erase   remove
16. _____ peek   ignore
17. _____ finish   end
18. _____ collapse   build
19. _____ wonder   know
20. _____ wonder   question

ACTIVITY 37 Define Words That Are Abstract Nouns

Name:_____

Date:_____

Words that name ideas are called **abstract nouns**. Something that is abstract cannot be touched. *Happiness* and *friendship* are abstract nouns.

Circle the word or words in each sentence that mean the same as the boldface word. Use a dictionary if you are not sure of the meaning of a word.

1. A person with **compassion** shows kindness to others.
2. To feel **fatigue** is to be very tired.
3. Beth's ability to paint was her greatest **talent**.
4. What is your recollection of your best **memory**?
5. If you make any more **mischief**, you will be in trouble for not behaving.
6. This **opportunity** is a chance you really should take.
7. If you **panic**, your fear will prevent you from being a success.
8. When someone forms an opinion without checking all the facts, she may learn that **prejudice** prevents her from having an open mind.
9. Angelo is curious about dinosaurs because he has an **interest** in them.
10. It is a **tradition** in the O'Connor family to hold a big celebration on St. Patrick's Day, a custom that began many, many years ago.

ACTIVITY 38 Relate Vocabulary Words to Personal Experiences

Name:_____

Date:_____

1. Describe a time when you felt compassion for someone. _____
   _____

2. Describe a family tradition. _____
   _____

3. Do you ever feel fatigue? _____ When? _____
   _____

4. Describe your best memory. _____
   _____

5. Give an example of prejudice. _____
   _____

6. Describe an opportunity you have had. _____
   _____

7. Give an example of a time when someone might panic. _____
   _____

8. Describe one of your talents. _____
   _____

ACTIVITY 39 Journal Writing

Name: _____

Date: _____

Write a journal entry about a memory or a family tradition that uses at least five words from the list. Underline the words you use.

compassion	fatigue	interest	memory	mischief
opportunity	panic	prejudice	talent	tradition

_____

_____

_____

_____

_____

_____

_____

_____

_____

ACTIVITY 40 Test-Taking

Name: _____

Date: _____

Write the letter of the answer that best matches the meaning of the word.

_____ 1. opportunity   a. win   b. chance   c. time   d. remember

_____ 2. interest   a. dislike   b. memory   c. museum   d. curiosity

_____ 3. prejudice   a. unfairness b. concern   c. kindness   d. tiredness

_____ 4. memory   a. old   b. recollection c. thought   d. ideas

_____ 5. fatigue   a. awake   b. asleep   c. tiredness   d. energy

_____ 6. mischief   a. trouble   b. fear   c. reward   d. danger

_____ 7. panic   a. anger   b. trouble   c. problem   d. fear

_____ 8. compassion   a. fear   b. anger   c. kindness   d. danger

_____ 9. talent   a. sports   b. ability   c. dancing   d. painting

_____ 10. tradition   a. Thanksgiving   b. family

                          c. feast   d. custom

ACTIVITY 41 Define Words That Are Verbs

Name:_____

Date:_____

Verbs are action words. All the words on this list are verbs. Use a dictionary to write a short definition for each verb.

1. accomplish _____
2. adjust _____
3. advance _____
4. advertise _____
5. amend _____
6. assign _____
7. embarrass _____
8. employ _____
9. equip _____
10. excite _____
11. improve _____
12. manage _____

ACTIVITY 42 Use Words in Context

Name:_____

Date:_____

Write the best word from the list to complete each sentence.

| accomplish | adjust | advance | advertise | amend | assign |
| embarrass | employ | equip | excite | improve | manage |

1. Before you go scuba diving, you'll need to _____ yourself with the right gear.
2. If you were a teacher, would you _____ homework?
3. Dad wants to _____ me to work in the garden this summer.
4. Do not _____ your little brother now, or he will not be able to sleep.
5. Will you _____ in the paper to sell your old bike?
6. How can you _____ your test scores?
7. In chess, the king can only _____ one space at a time.
8. Phil worked to _____ the law because he felt it was wrong.
9. Will you be able to _____ all the gear alone?
10. You can _____ much if you work hard.
11. You will _____ Tammy if you mention her purple hair.
12. Can you _____ the water temperature so it is not so hot?

21

ACTIVITY 43 Write and Use the Past Tense of Verbs in Context

Name:_____

Date:_____

Past tense means something happened before now.

Example: Jerry fumbled the ball, and our team lost the game.

For most verbs, add *-ed* to form the past tense. When verbs end in "*e*," drop the "*e*" before adding the *-ed*. On another sheet of paper, use the past tense of each verb in a sentence. Use a dictionary if you need help.

1. accomplish
2. adjust
3. advance
4. advertise
5. amend
6. assign

7. embarrass
8. employ
9. equip
10. excite
11. improve
12. manage

ACTIVITY 44 Test-Taking

Name:_____

Date:_____

Circle "T" for true or "F" for false.

1. T F To **accomplish** means to finish a job.
2. T F To **advertise** means to promote something or offer something for sale.
3. T F To **embarrass** is to make someone very happy.
4. T F To **excite** means to feel sad.
5. T F To **manage** means to get married.
6. T F To **improve** means to get better.
7. T F To **employ** means to hire someone or to use a tool.
8. T F To **amend** means to buy something new.
9. T F To **adjust** means to make a change.
10. T F To **assign** means to give someone a task.
11. T F To **equip** means to gather the right supplies for a task or outing.
12. T F To **advance** means to move backward.

ACTIVITY 45 Define Words That Are Nouns

Name: _____

Date: _____

Nouns are words that name people, places, things, or ideas. Match the words with their definitions. Use a dictionary if you are not sure of the meaning of a word.

_____	1. accomplishment	a.	movement forward or higher
_____	2. adjustment	b.	a change or addition to a document, rule, or policy
_____	3. advancement	c.	a feeling of shame
_____	4. advertisement	d.	a correction
_____	5. amendment	e.	a deed that has been done
_____	6. assignment	f.	a thrill
_____	7. embarrassment	g.	a change that makes something work better
_____	8. employment	h.	supplies needed
_____	9. equipment	i.	a task or job given to someone
_____	10. excitement	j.	work for pay
_____	11. improvement	k.	owners or bosses
_____	12. management	l.	an announcement of something for sale

FOR SALE: 6-foot green iguana with cage. Very friendly, great pet. Call 555-5555.

ACTIVITY 46 Determine Root Words

Name: _____

Date: _____

A **suffix** is added at the end of a word. It changes the meaning of the word. Sometimes it changes the spelling of the root word.

When the suffix *-ment* is added to a verb, it changes the <u>verb</u> to a <u>noun</u>. Sometimes the spelling of the verb changes.

Write the verb that is the root word for each noun.

1. accomplishment _____
2. advancement _____
3. amendment _____
4. embarrassment _____
5. equipment _____
6. improvement _____

7. adjustment _____
8. advertisement _____
9. assignment _____
10. employment _____
11. excitement _____
12. management _____

Adjustment, *amendment*, and *improvement* all mean to change something, but the words do not mean the same thing. On the back of this page, use each word in a sentence that shows you understand the meaning of these three words. Use a dictionary if you are unsure.

13. adjustment   14. amendment   15. improvement

ACTIVITY 47 Relate Vocabulary Words to Personal Life

Name: _____

Date: _____

Answer the following questions on another sheet of paper.

1. What do you feel is your greatest accomplishment?
2. What adjustment would you like to make to your wardrobe (clothes you wear)?
3. What qualities do you think are important for people who are in management?
4. Write an advertisement to sell something unusual.
5. What is your favorite type of homework assignment?
6. How do you feel about people who cause you embarrassment?
7. What type of employment would you like to have someday?
8. What equipment do you need for your hobby?
9. Describe some excitement you've had lately.
10. What improvement would you most like to make in your life?

Did you know? The first ten amendments to the Constitution are called the Bill of Rights.

ACTIVITY 48 Test-Taking

Name: _____

Date: _____

Circle "T" for true or "F" for false.

1. T F To complete a job correctly is an **accomplishment**.
2. T F **Adjustments** are changes to fix something so it works better.
3. T F **Advancement** is another word for progress.
4. T F All **advertisements** offer items for free.
5. T F An **amendment** is an addition to a movie.
6. T F A homework **assignment** is always very difficult.
7. T F Most people are not bothered by **embarrassment**.
8. T F **Employment** is work for pay.
9. T F **Equipment** means clothing you wear to school every day.
10. T F **Excitement** means a boring vacation.
11. T F A change that makes something better is an **improvement**.
12. T F People in **management** are in charge of others.

ACTIVITY 49 Define Words That Are Verbs

Name:_____

Date:_____

Verbs are actions words. All the words on this list are verbs. Some of the words are also nouns. Write the words from the list to match their definitions. Use a dictionary if you are not sure of the meaning of a word.

accelerate	amplify	attempt	defend	delay
fumble	modify	occupy	roam	summarize

1. _____ to change
2. _____ to live in
3. _____ to protect
4. _____ to sum up
5. _____ to cause to be late

6. _____ to drop
7. _____ to make louder
8. _____ to speed up
9. _____ to try
10. _____ to wander

Many verbs can be changed to nouns. *Example: Accelerate* means to go fast. The pedal in a car that makes it go faster is called the *accelerator*. Answer the questions below on your own paper. Use a dictionary if you are not sure of the meaning of a word.

11. What does an amplifier do? What is the root word?
12. What is an occupant? What is the root word?

13. What is a summary?
14. What is a modification?

ACTIVITY 50 Differentiate Between Noun and Verb Use of Words

Name:_____

Date:_____

Use a dictionary if you need help writing the sentences.

1. Use *delay* as a verb in a sentence. _____

   _____

2. Use *delay* as a noun in a sentence. _____

   _____

3. Use *fumble* as a verb in a sentence. _____

   _____

4. Use *fumble* as a noun in a sentence. _____

   _____

5. Use *attempt* as a verb in a sentence. _____

   _____

6. Use *attempt* as a noun in a sentence. _____

   _____

ACTIVITY 51   Write Antonyms, Synonyms, and Questions

Name:_____

Date:_____

Antonyms are words that mean the opposite. Write an antonym for each word.

1. accelerate _____
2. fumble _____
3. defend _____
4. roam _____

Synonyms are words the mean the same or nearly the same. Write a synonym for each word.

5. amplify _____
6. delay _____
7. occupy _____
8. attempt _____
9. modify _____
10. summarize _____

Sentences that ask a question end with a question mark. Many questions begin with *who, what, when, where, why,* or *how.* Write a question sentence for each word.

11. accelerate _____
12. amplify _____
13. defend _____
14. occupy _____
15. roam _____

ACTIVITY 52   Test-Taking

Name:_____

Date:_____

Write the letter of the answer that best matches the definition.

_____ 1. summarize
    a. a short story   b. to sum up   c. a report   d. to write a report

_____ 2. roam
    a. to march   b. to sleepwalk   c. to wander   d. a city in Italy

_____ 3. amplify
    a. to make louder   b. speakers   c. music   d. a sound

_____ 4. fumble
    a. to catch   b. to throw   c. a football   d. to drop

_____ 5. occupy
    a. to live in   b. to leave   c. to rent   d. a person who rents

_____ 6. attempt
    a. to do   b. to fail   c. to try   d. to succeed

_____ 7. defend
    a. to attack   b. to live in a fort   c. a castle   d. to protect

_____ 8. accelerate
    a. to slow down   b. to go faster   c. pedal on a car   d. to race

_____ 9. delay
    a. prevent   b. to cause to be late   c. to be on time   d. wait and see

_____ 10. modify
    a. to paint   b. to decorate   c. to look closely   d. to change

ACTIVITY 53   Write Antonyms and Synonyms for Review Words

Name:_____

Date:_____

Write an antonym for each word.

1. accelerate _____
2. collapse _____
3. depart _____
4. erase _____
5. finish _____
6. reply _____
7. shiver _____

8. advance _____
9. delay _____
10. employ _____
11. fatigue _____
12. improve _____
13. rescue _____
14. wonder _____

Write a synonym for each word.

15. accomplish _____
16. amend _____
17. carnival _____
18. defend _____
19. garment _____
20. opportunity _____
21. peek _____

22. adjust _____
23. attempt _____
24. compassion _____
25. fabric _____
26. mischief _____
27. pebbles _____
28. wander _____

ACTIVITY 54   Differentiate Between Nouns and Verbs

Name:_____

Date:_____

Write "N" if the word is a noun. Write "V" if the word is a verb.

1. _____ accomplishment
2. _____ amendment
3. _____ embarrass
4. _____ equip
5. _____ foundation
6. _____ management
7. _____ platform
8. _____ roam
9. _____ talent

10. _____ advertise
11. _____ assign
12. _____ employment
13. _____ excite
14. _____ manage
15. _____ memory
16. _____ prejudice
17. _____ summarize
18. _____ tradition

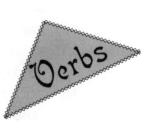

ACTIVITY 55 Write the Past Tense of Verbs

Name: _____

Date: _____

Write the past tense of each verb.

1. adjust   _____
2. equip   _____
3. improve   _____
4. amend   _____
5. collapse   _____
6. depart   _____
7. erase   _____
8. finish   _____
9. peek   _____
10. rescue   _____

11. shiver   _____
12. wander   _____
13. wonder   _____
14. accomplish _____
15. advance   _____

PLAY _____

ACTIVITY 56 Define Review Words

Name: _____

Date: _____

Match the words with their definitions.

_____ 1. advancement
_____ 2. advertisement
_____ 3. amendment
_____ 4. amplify
_____ 5. assignment
_____ 6. defend
_____ 7. delay
_____ 8. equipment
_____ 9. excitement
_____ 10. foundation
_____ 11. fumble
_____ 12. improvement
_____ 13. ingredients
_____ 14. modify
_____ 15. occupy
_____ 16. prescription
_____ 17. roam

a. to drop
b. to protect
c. supplies needed
d. movement forward or higher
e. a thrill
f. to wander
g. a change that makes something work better
h. a task or job given to someone
i. parts used to make something such as cookies
j. to make louder
k. a change or addition to a document, rule, or policy
l. medicine ordered by a doctor
m. an announcement of something wanted or for sale
n. to change
o. to cause to be late
p. the base of something
q. to live in

Freedom of speech

ACTIVITY 57   Define Words With Multiple Meanings

Name:_____

Date:_____

Many words have more than one meaning. Write the word from the list that matches the definition. Each word will be used more than once. Use a dictionary if you are not sure of the meaning of a word.

catalog	crop	deposit	experience	grasp
offer	protest	purchase	sketch	stall

1. a drawing _____
2. a listing _____
3. a bid _____
4. to cut off part _____
5. to buy _____
6. to grab _____
7. a firm hold _____
8. to list _____
9. to suggest _____
10. to object _____

11. prior knowledge _____
12. a horse's place in a barn _____
13. an objection _____
14. money put in a bank _____
15. plant grown for food _____
16. something bought _____
17. to draw quickly _____
18. to put money in a bank _____
19. to live an event _____
20. to put off until later _____

ACTIVITY 58   Use Words in Context

Name:_____

Date:_____

Write words from the list to complete the sentences. Words can be used more than once.

catalog	crop	deposit	experience	grasp
offer	protest	purchase	sketch	stall

1. _____ the picture before you make a copy to get rid of the fuzzy edges.
2. Can I _____ you some help?
3. Can you _____ the rope if I move it closer?
4. Will you _____ that mountain so I can remember how it looked?
5. Did you _____ a swim in the icy water?
6. How much money did you _____ last time?
7. I bought six movies from a mail-order _____.
8. I said I would _____ if he took my car.
9. If you _____ any longer, it will be too late to go.
10. My horse is in the first _____ in the barn.
11. My only _____ was a dill pickle.
12. Who did that great _____ of your dog?
13. We received an _____ to buy our old car.

ACTIVITY 59 Use Words in Context/ Write a Description

Name: _____

Date: _____

Write a description of an experience you've had. It can be real or imaginary. Use at least six words from the list.

| catalog | crop | deposit | experience | grasp |
| offer | protest | purchase | sketch | stall |

_____

_____

_____

_____

_____

_____

_____

_____

_____

_____

ACTIVITY 60 Test-Taking

Name: _____

Date: _____

Circle "T" for true or "F" for false.

1. T F A **catalog** is a book of maps.
2. T F A **sketch** is a finished painting.
3. T F An **offer** is a plan for building a new house.
4. T F Some animals are kept in **stalls**.
5. T F Cars are an important type of **crop** in the United States.
6. T F If someone **crops** your hair, it will be shorter.
7. T F If you **purchase** something, you need to pay for it.
8. T F If you **stall** too long, you could be late.
9. T F Money is the only thing you can **deposit**.
10. T F Something free is a **purchase**.
11. T F To **catalog** means to list items.
12. T F To **deposit** means to get money from a bank.
13. T F To **sketch** something means to draw it quickly.
14. T F When you **experience** something, you watch someone else.
15. T F When you **grasp** something, you let it go.
16. T F When you **protest** something, it means you agree with it.

ACTIVITY 61 Define Words That Are Adjectives

Name:_____

Date:_____

Adjectives are words that describe nouns. *Example:* The rusty, old, red car broke down on the dusty gravel road. *Rusty*, *old*, and *red* describe the car. *Dusty* and *gravel* describe the road. All the words on the list below are adjectives. Write the adjective from the list to match its definition. Use a dictionary if you are not sure of the meaning of a word.

> awkward   circular   delicious   diagonal   essential
> generous   gigantic   gorgeous   severe   slender

1. _____ thin
2. _____ important; necessary
3. _____ huge
4. _____ round
5. _____ very pretty; good-looking
6. _____ stern
7. _____ tasty
8. _____ not graceful; clumsy
9. _____ kind; giving
10. _____ a line drawn from corner to corner of a square or rectangle; at an angle

ACTIVITY 62 Use Adjectives in Context

Name:_____

Date:_____

Write words from the list to complete the sentences.

> awkward   circular   delicious   diagonal   essential
> generous   gigantic   gorgeous   severe   slender

1. A peacock has _____ tail feathers.

2. Aunt Sarah's cream puffs are the most _____ food you could ever eat.

3. Clark found a _____ mushroom in his backyard.

4. The long, _____ stem of the flower swayed in the wind.

5. In chess, the bishop can only move in a _____ direction.

6. Many people think cell phones are _____ tools.

7. Mason's _____ gift to the museum provided for many new exhibits.

8. Penguins look _____ when they walk but are very graceful in the water.

9. Schools were closed after the _____ blizzard.

10. We climbed the _____ staircase to the top of the lighthouse.

ACTIVITY 63 Write Causes and Effects   Name:_____

Date:_____

Finish each sentence by writing a cause.

1. The colt was awkward because _____
   _____

2. We walked across the field at a diagonal because _____
   _____

3. The only reason the mushroom was so gigantic was because _____
   _____

Finish each sentence by writing an effect.

5. _____
   _____ due to the severe storm.

6. _____
   _____ because it was necessary for his business.

7. Because Art's painting was so gorgeous, _____
   _____

8. After we climbed the circular staircase, _____
   _____

ACTIVITY 64 Test-Taking   Name:_____

Date:_____

Write the letter of the answer that is an antonym for the word listed.

1. _____ generous   a. kind   b. giving   c. cheap   d. pretty

2. _____ circular   a. round   b. spiral   c. crooked   d. straight

3. _____ diagonal   a. round   b. straight   c. angled   d. square

4. _____ slender   a. thin   b. narrow   c. wide   d. skinny

5. _____ delicious   a. great   b. yummy   c. bad-tasting d. super

6. _____ essential   a. needed   b. unnecessary   c. required   d. easy

7. _____ gigantic   a. huge   b. large   c. big   d. tiny

8. _____ awkward   a. clumsy   b. graceful   c. rough   d. unhappy

9. _____ gorgeous   a. beautiful b. pretty   c. nice   d. ugly

10. _____ severe   a. kind   b. extreme   c. cruel   d. strict

ACTIVITY 65 Define Words/ Add Prefixes

Name:_____

Date:_____

Adjectives are words that describe nouns. All of the words on this list are adjectives. Write the words from the list to match their definitions. Use a dictionary if you are not sure of the meaning of a word.

appropriate	capable	possible	practical	proper	sincere

1. _____ likely

2. _____ suitable

3. _____ able

4. _____ correct

5. _____ truthful; open

6. _____ useful or handy

When a prefix is added to the beginning of a word, it changes the meaning of the word. The prefixes *im-* and *in-* change the meaning of a word to its opposite.

Examples: formal – informal   movable – immovable

Add *in-* or *im-* to each word below to form a new word. Use a dictionary if you are not sure which prefix to add.

7. appropriate _____

8. equality _____

9. flexible _____

10. capable _____

11. possible _____

12. practical _____

END SLAVERY

ACTIVITY 66 Relate Vocabulary Words to Personal Experience

Name:_____

Date:_____

1. Give an example of an appropriate action. _____

2. Give an example of an inappropriate action. _____

3. Name two things you are capable of doing. _____

4. Name one thing you are incapable of doing. _____

5. Give an example of equality. _____

6. Give an example of inequality. _____

7. Name something that is flexible. _____

8. Name something that is inflexible. _____

9. Name something that is possible for you. _____

10. Name something that is impossible for you. _____

11. Give an example of a sincere action. _____

12. Give an example of an insincere action. _____

ACTIVITY 67 Use Words in Context

Name: _____

Date: _____

Circle the correct word in each sentence.

1. A gymnast is very (flexible / inflexible).
2. A person who is (sincere / insincere) will probably not have many friends.
3. It is (proper / improper) to thank someone for a gift.
4. A rock is very (flexible / inflexible).
5. When people are treated unfairly, it is a sign of (equality / inequality).
6. When someone is (sincere / insincere), they are truthful and open.
7. Most people are (capable / incapable) of holding their breath for three minutes.
8. It is (appropriate / inappropriate) to sing loudly in the library.
9. It is (possible / impossible) to walk across the United States.
10. It is (practical / impractical) to walk across the United States.
11. It is (proper / improper) to burp at the table.
12. Not everyone is (capable / incapable) of being a great athlete.

ACTIVITY 68 Test-Taking

Name: _____

Date: _____

Write the letter of the answer that best matches the definition for each word.

1. _____ appropriate   a. suitable   b. unable   c. not suitable   d. fair
2. _____ capable   a. fair   b. strong   c. unable   d. able
3. _____ equality   a. unfair   b. fairness   c. unjust   d. suitable
4. _____ flexible   a. weak   b. heavy   c. strong   d. bendable
5. _____ impossible   a. likely   b. can't happen   c. for sure   d. certain
6. _____ impractical   a. useful   b. not useful   c. wrong   d. to sing
7. _____ improper   a. right   b. incorrect   c. correct   d. burping
8. _____ inappropriate   a. okay   b. unsuitable   c. not happy   d. suitable
9. _____ incapable   a. clever   b. smart   c. unable   d. able
10. _____ inequality   a. fairness   b. unfairness   c. unhappy   d. dishonest
11. _____ inflexible   a. movable   b. changing   c. weak   d. hard; firm
12. _____ insincere   a. truthful   b. honest   c. wrong   d. not truthful
13. _____ possible   a. rare   b. likely   c. unlikely   d. often
14. _____ practical   a. not useful   b. thankful   c. useful   d. kind
15. _____ proper   a. useful   b. not correct   c. wrong   d. correct

ACTIVITY 69 Define Compound Words

Name: _____

Date: _____

A **compound word** combines two or more words to make a new word that expresses a single idea. Sometimes the meaning of the new word isn't clear, even though you know the meaning of both words used. Use a dictionary if you need help answering the questions on your own paper.

1. A **crossover** is where you cross from one place to another. Where can you find a crossover?

2. If you know something **firsthand**, it means that you know it because you have done it or seen it for yourself. Something someone else tells you is called secondhand information. Give an example of something you know firsthand.

3. A **hardship** doesn't have anything to do with a boat. It means a problem or difficulty. Use *hardship* in a sentence.

4. The physical parts of a computer, like the keyboard and monitor, are called **hardware**. However, you would not go to a hardware store to buy a computer. What could you buy in a hardware store?

5. When you travel by airplane, you sometimes have a **layover**. What is a *layover*?

6. An **overview** means a summary of a situation or problem. Why do you think the words *over* and *view* were combined for this meaning?

7. If someone is a **pushover**, it does not mean he or she falls over easily. What does *pushover* mean?

8. Many people feel sorry for someone who is an **underdog**. What is an *underdog*?

- -

ACTIVITY 70 Identify Compound Words

Name: _____

Date: _____

Make a copy of a page of a newspaper or magazine. Find and circle all the compound words on the page. List the compound words you found.

_____

_____

_____

_____

_____

_____

_____

_____

_____

_____

_____

ACTIVITY 71 Use Compound Words in Context

Name: _____

Date: _____

It is necessary to know when to use a compound word and when to use the two words separately. You can do this by carefully reading the sentence.

Circle the correct word or words in each sentence.

1. Please do not (cross over / crossover) the floor until it dries.
2. If you put your (first hand / firsthand) on the ladder, you can reach the top with your other hand.
3. A voyage at sea was not a (hard ship / hardship) for Captain Ahab.
4. Will you have a (lay over / layover) in Chicago on your way to Seattle?
5. Please give me an (over view / overview) of the problem, so I can understand it better.
6. Be careful or you will (push over / pushover) the lamp with your foot.
7. Would you like your (roll over / rollover) here or in the kitchen?
8. Everyone cheered for the (under dog / underdog).
9. The (under study / understudy) was a better actor than the star.
10. I bought new (hard ware / hardware) and tools at the store.

ACTIVITY 72 Test-Taking

Name: _____

Date: _____

Write the letter of the answer that would best replace the **** in each sentence.

1. _____ If you need new **** for your computer, I know a great place to shop.
   a. programs   b. hard ware   c. hardware   d. tools
2. _____ She gained **** experience while climbing mountains in Colorado.
   a. secondhand   b. firsthand   c. first hand   d. handsome
3. _____ Grandma is a ****. She will say "yes" to anything.
   a. rollover   b. turnover   c. crossover   d. pushover
4. _____ Two people were hurt in the **** accident.
   a. rollover   b. roll over   c. injury   d. overturn
5. _____ In winter, it is a **** if the power goes out.
   a. hardware   b. hardship   c. friendship   d. hard ship
6. _____ We walked to the **** before trying to cross Main Street.
   a. sidewalk   b. bridge   c. crossover   d. street
7. _____ Our **** lasted two hours longer than we expected.
   a. turnover   b. carryover   c. overlay   d. layover
8. _____ When he was lost, Todd climbed a tree to get an **** of the area.
   a. review   b. preview   c. overview   d. interview
9. _____ The director called the **** to perform when the star broke his leg.
   a. audience   b. understudy   c. doctor   d. theater

ACTIVITY 73 Define Words With the Prefixes "un-" or "dis-"

Name:_____

Date:_____

When a prefix is added to the beginning of a word, it changes the meaning of the word. The prefixes *dis-* and *un-* change the meaning of a word to its opposite.

Examples: respect – disrespect   common – uncommon

Add *dis-* or *un-* to each boldface word to form a new word. Use a dictionary if you are not sure which prefix to add. Then, on another sheet of paper, write a sentence using each new word.

1. To **agree** means to have the same opinion. New word = _____
2. **Available** means something can be had or is near. New word = _____
3. A **belief** is faith or trust in someone or something. New word = _____
4. **Believable** means something makes sense. It is realistic. New word =

   _____

5. To **continue** means to carry on as before. New word = _____
6. **Desirable** means pleasing. New word = _____
7. **Honest** means worthy of trust or one who does not lie. New word = _____
8. **Known** means something of which you are aware. New word = _____
9. **Limited** means partial or not complete. New word = _____
10. **Necessary** means something important or needed. New word = _____

ACTIVITY 74 Use Words in Context

Name:_____

Date:_____

Write a word from the list to complete each sentence.

agree	available	belief	believable	continue	desirable
disagree	disbelief	discontinue	dishonest	honest	known
limited	necessary	unavailable	unbelievable	undesirable	unknown

1. The amount I can spend is _____ because I do not have very much.
2. "I'm sorry," said the librarian. "The movie you wanted is _____."
3. "I strongly _____!" shouted Ted, "I will not vote for your idea."
4. That's _____!" the coach told Sal. He looked at her in

   _____. "No one can run 100 miles an hour."
5. Of all the people I have ever _____, Tina is the most

   _____. I would trust her with anything.
6. Is it really _____ to burp every time you drink root beer?
7. The most _____ seats in the gym were in the front

   row, close to the action.
8. "The blouse you wanted is _____ in blue only. We had to

   _____ all other colors," said the clerk.

ACTIVITY 75 Use Words in Context/ Write Dialogue

Name: _____

Date: _____

Write a conversation between two people who disagree on something. Continue on another sheet of paper. Use as many of the words from the list as possible.

agree	disagree	available	unavailable	belief	disbelief
believable	unbelievable	continue	discontinue	desirable	undesirable
encourage	discourage	honest	dishonest	known	unknown
limited	unlimited	necessary	unnecessary		

She said, "_____."

He said, "_____."

She said, "_____."

He said, "_____."

She said, "_____."

He said, "_____."

She said, "_____."

He said, "_____."

ACTIVITY 76 Test-Taking

Name: _____

Date: _____

Write the letter of the answer that best matches the meaning of the definition.

1. _____ cannot be obtained   a. believable   b. available   c. unavailable

2. _____ lack of faith or trust   a. belief   b. disbelief   c. unavailable

3. _____ not needed   a. necessary   b. dishonest   c. unnecessary

4. _____ not truthful   a. dishonest   b. honest   c. disbelief

5. _____ unwanted   a. desirable   b. unbelievable   c. undesirable

6. _____ makes sense   a. disbelief   b. believable   c. unbelievable

7. _____ something of which you are aware   a. necessary   b. known   c. unknown

8. _____ to have the same opinion   a. agree   b. believable   c. disagree

9. _____ to stop something   a. unavailable   b. continue   c. discontinue

10. _____ without end   a. limited   b. unlimited   c. unnecessary

ACTIVITY 77 Define Words That Are Nouns

Name:_____

Date:_____

Nouns are words that name people, places, things, or ideas. All the words on this list are nouns. Match the words with their definitions. Use a dictionary if you are not sure of the meaning of a word.

1. _____ auditorium   a. a smell
2. _____ bachelor   b. the winner
3. _____ cavern   c. someone who sells things
4. _____ champion   d. a place where crops are grown
5. _____ conflict   e. a large cave
6. _____ duty   f. a disagreement
7. _____ field   g. a win
8. _____ fragrance   h. a task to be done
9. _____ merchant   i. a man who is not married
10. _____ museum   j. a device that fills with air when jumping from an airplane
11. _____ parachute   k. a place where people can view old, rare, or special things
12. _____ victory   l. a large room used for public meetings or performances

13. Write another definition for *field*. _____

- -

ACTIVITY 78 Classify Words That Are Nouns

Name:_____

Date:_____

Write the words from the list that fit in each group. Add two other nouns of your own for each group.

| auditorium | field | museum | conflict | duty | fragrance |
| victory | bachelor | champion | merchant | cavern | parachute |

Persons	**Places**	**Things**	**Ideas**
_____	_____	_____	_____
_____	_____	_____	_____
_____	_____	_____	_____
_____	_____	_____	_____
_____	_____	_____	_____
_____	_____	_____	_____

What is your favorite museum? _____ What types of things are at that museum?

_____

ACTIVITY 79   Determine Facts or Opinions   Name:_____

Date:_____

Circle "F" for fact or "O" for opinion.

1.   F   O   An **auditorium** is a great place to play.
2.   F   O   A football **field** is larger than a basketball court.
3.   F   O   Natural history **museums** are more interesting than art museums.
4.   F   O   Exploring a **cavern** would be a great way to spend a Saturday.
5.   F   O   **Conflict** should always be avoided.
6.   F   O   Doing one's **duty** is not important.
7.   F   O   Some flowers have a sweet **fragrance**.
8.   F   O   Only the winner will achieve a **victory**.
9.   F   O   A **bachelor** is a man who is not married.
10.   F   O   Every **champion** is a great athlete.
11.   F   O   **Merchants** care more about making money than the quality of products.
12.   F   O   **Parachuting** is a fun sport.

On another sheet of paper, write the following.

13.   Write a fact about your school.
14.   Write an opinion about your school.

ACTIVITY 80   Test-Taking

Name:_____

Date:_____

Write the letter of the answer that best matches the definition for each word.

1.   _____   auditorium   a. a large cave   b. a place where plants are grown
                          c. a hearing aid   d. a large room; a gym
2.   _____   cavern   a. a theater   b. a large cave
                          c. a small room   d. a place to grow crops
3.   _____   field   a. a forest   b. a smooth lake
                          c. a playground   d. a place where crops are grown
4.   _____   museum   a. an auditorium   b. a castle
                          c. a junk store   d. a place to view special things
5.   _____   conflict   a. to make peace   b. a disagreement
                          c. final   d. to speak loudly
6.   _____   duty   a. a task to be done   b. trusting
                          c. kindness   d. school
7.   _____   fragrance   a. perfume   b. flowers
                          c. a bakery   d. garden
8.   _____   victory   a. champion   b. success
                          c. defeat   d. a musical instrument
9.   _____   bachelor   a. a young boy   b. a woman who is not married
                          c. a married person   d. a man who is not married

ACTIVITY 81   Review/Classify Nouns

Name:_____

Date:_____

Write the nouns from the list that fit into each group.

auditorium	bachelor	belief	catalog	cavern	champion	conflict
crop	crossover	customer	deposit	duty	experience	field
fragrance	hardship	hardware	honesty	honor	merchant	museum
offer	overview	parachute	protest	purchase	pushover	rollover
sketch	stall	talent	underdog	understudy		

People _____

_____

Places _____

_____

Things _____

_____

Ideas _____

_____

ACTIVITY 82   Write Compound Words

Name:_____

Date:_____

Some plants and animals have names that are compound words.

Examples: bulldog, firefly, swordfish, butterfly, dogwood, pineapple, strawberry

1. Use any reference sources to find ten or more animals or plants with compound word names. _____

_____

_____

_____

2. Many places have compound word names such as *Maryland*, *Deerfield*, *Iceland*, and *Hollywood*. Use an atlas or other reference source to find ten or more places with compound word names. _____

_____

_____

_____

3. Select three places with compound word names. On another sheet of paper, make up a reason why those places may have been given their names.

ACTIVITY 83 Review Adjectives/ Write Nouns

Name:_____

Date:_____

Write two nouns that could be described by each adjective. The first one has been done as an example.

1. awkward ___*fall, moment*___   2. capable _____

3. circular _____   4. delicious_____

5. diagonal_____   6. essential _____

7. flexible_____   8. generous _____

9. gigantic _____   10. gorgeous _____

11. impossible _____   12. impractical _____

13. inappropriate _____   14. incapable _____

15. inflexible_____   16. insincere _____

17. possible _____   18. practical _____

19. proper _____   20. severe _____

ACTIVITY 84 Define Review Words

Name:_____

Date:_____

Write the words from the list to match the definitions. Some words may be used more than once.

awkward	capable	catalog	conflict	crop	delicious	equality
essential	experience	flexible	fragrance	generous	merchant	proper
protest	severe	sincere	sketch	stall	victory	

1. _____ a win   2. _____ a drawing

3. _____ a listing   4. _____ a smell

5. _____ able   6. _____ bends easily

7. _____ fairness   8. _____ important

9. _____ tasty   10. _____ stern

11. _____ suitable   12. _____ to list

13. _____ to object   14. _____ truthful

15. _____ a disagreement   16. _____ an objection

17. _____ correct   18. _____ kind; giving

19. _____ not graceful; clumsy   20. _____ prior knowledge

21. _____ a seller   22. _____ to cut off part

23. _____ to draw quickly   24. _____ to live an event

25. _____ to put off until later 26. _____ plants for food

42

ACTIVITY 85 Define Adjectives

Name:_____

Date:_____

Adjectives are words that describe nouns, such as *anxious*, *frigid*, and *rapid*. All the words on this list are adjectives. Write the word from the list that means the same as the underlined words in each sentence. Use a dictionary if you are not sure of the meaning of a word.

actual	exact	former	instant
keen	natural	regular	visual

1. _____ The latest movie had many great effects <u>you could see</u>.
2. _____ Do you know the <u>precise</u> cost of the repairs for your car?
3. _____ The drummer kept up a <u>steady</u> beat on the bass drum.
4. _____ We have an <u>immediate</u> need for a fire extinguisher.
5. _____ Her sense of smell was very <u>sharp and clear</u>.
6. _____ The <u>previous</u> coach also taught math classes.
7. _____ This painting is a copy; the <u>real</u> Mona Lisa is in Paris.
8. _____ Geoff preferred to eat vegetables that were <u>produced by nature</u> rather than ones canned in a factory.

ACTIVITY 86 Write Adjectives to Describe Nouns

Name:_____

Date:_____

Adjectives describe nouns. For each noun, write an adjective from the list that could describe it. Words may be used more than once. Use each word at least once.

actual	annual	exact	former	gradual	instant
keen	natural	regular	typical	usual	visual

1. _____ answer   2. _____ behavior
3. _____ belief   4. _____ decline
5. _____ effect   6. _____ event
7. _____ eyesight   8. _____ job
9. _____ manner   10. _____ novel
11. _____ parade   12. _____ pattern
13. _____ president   14. _____ problems
15. _____ sense   16. _____ success
17. _____ teacher   18. _____ time
19. _____ weather   20. _____ wonder

ACTIVITY 87 Use Words in Context/ Write Sentences

Name: _____

Date: _____

Write sentences using all of the words on the list. You can use more than one word per sentence. Underline the words from the list.

actual	annual	exact	former	gradual	instant
keen	natural	regular	typical	usual	visual

_____

_____

_____

_____

_____

_____

_____

_____

_____

ACTIVITY 88 Test-Taking

Name: _____

Date: _____

Write the letter of the answer that best matches the meaning of the word.

1. _____ typical   a. unusual   b. normal   c. timely   d. odd

2. _____ annual   a. monthly   b. daily   c. yearly   d. seldom

3. _____ instant   a. immediate   b. later   c. gradual   d. slow

4. _____ exact   a. about   b. close   c. vague   d. precise

5. _____ former   a. later   b. new   c. previous   d. lasting

6. _____ visual   a. heard   b. seen   c. touched   d. smelled

7. _____ gradual   a. instant   b. quick   c. steadily   d. seldom

8. _____ usual   a. same   b. exact   c. unusual   d. different

9. _____ natural   a. produced   b. cooked   c. fruit   d. not artificial

10. _____ actual   a. gradual   b. real   c. typical   d. copy

11. _____ regular   a. steady   b. firm   c. unsteady   d. different

12. _____ keen   a. seen   b. sharp   c. dull   d. bright

ACTIVITY 89 Define Adverbs

Name:_____

Date:_____

Adverbs are used with verbs, adjectives, or other adverbs to describe, limit, or make the meaning of the word clearer. Adding a **suffix** to a word changes the meaning of the word. Adding the suffix *-ly* to an <u>adjective</u> can change it to an <u>adverb</u>.

  Examples: Fierce and *gentle* are <u>adjectives</u>. *Fiercely* and *gently* are <u>adverbs</u>.

Write the adjective form of each word. Then write a short definition for the adverb. Use a dictionary if you need help. The first one has been done as an example.

	Adjective	Adverb	Definition of Adverb
1.	*actual*	actually	*in fact*
2.	_____	annually	_____
3.	_____	exactly	_____
4.	_____	formerly	_____
5.	_____	gradually	_____
6.	_____	instantly	_____
7.	_____	keenly	_____
8.	_____	naturally	_____

ACTIVITY 90 Use Adverbs in Context

Name:_____

Date:_____

Adverbs clarify meaning in a sentence by answering the questions *why, where, when, how,* or *to what extent.* Underline the adverb in each sentence. Write the question it answers.

  Example: Taxes are due <u>annually</u> by April 15.

    Annually is an adverb. It answers <u>when</u> taxes are due.

1. The total for the repairs came to exactly $712.14. _____

2. Formerly we had planned to go to Paris, but we changed our minds.

   _____

3. Paul gradually increased the number of miles he jogged each day. _____

4. The trees grew naturally in the forest. _____

5. We regularly take walks in the woods. _____

6. Typically, we walk for about an hour. _____

7. Usually, our dog, Max, goes with us. _____

8. Rachel keenly looks forward to our walks. _____

9. In fall, the forest is visually delightful. _____

10. Actually, I like walking in winter best of all. _____

11. We gather hickory nuts annually. _____

ACTIVITY 91 Use Adverbs in Context/
Write a News Article

Name:_____

Date:_____

A good news article answers the questions *who*, *what*, *when*, *where*, *why*, and *how*. Write a short news article to go with the headline below. Use at least six words from the list.

actually	annually	exactly	formerly	gradually	instantly
keenly	naturally	regularly	typically	usually	visually

CHANGES IN SCHOOL POLICY ANNOUNCED

_____ _____
_____ _____
_____ _____
_____ _____
_____ _____
_____ _____
_____ _____
_____ _____

ACTIVITY 92 Test-Taking

Name:_____

Date:_____

Write the letter of the answer that best matches the word.

1. _____ exactly   a. vaguely   b. precisely   c. about   d. almost
2. _____ usually   a. most often   b. seldom   c. rarely   d. never
3. _____ formerly   a. currently   b. before now   c. later   d. right now
4. _____ typically   a. timely   b. sometimes   c. usually   d. never
5. _____ gradually   a. quickly   b. regularly   c. soon   d. slowly
6. _____ regularly   a. seldom   b. sometimes   c. firmly   d. on a regular basis
7. _____ instantly   a. pretty soon   b. at once   c. for a while d. frequently
8. _____ keenly   a. kindly   b. visually   c. sharply   d. strongly
9. _____ annually   a. yearly   b. monthly   c. daily   d. hourly
10. _____ visually   a. with ears   b. with sight   c. with touch   d. with smell
11. _____ naturally   a. crookedly   b. lately   c. soon   d. not artificially
12. _____ actually   a. perhaps   b. maybe   c. in fact   d. before now

ACTIVITY 93 **Define Geography Words** Name:_____

Date:_____

Use a dictionary or other reference source to answer the questions.

1. *Aqua* means *water* in Latin. The Romans were famous for building aqueducts. What is an *aqueduct*? _____

2. On a map, the boundary between two states or two countries is marked with a line. If you cross a *boundary* between two states, will you be able to see the line? _____

3. *Glaciers* are huge accumulations of ice, snow, water, rock, and sediment that move slowly because of gravity. Glaciers form when temperatures are low enough to allow snow to accumulate and slowly transform into ice. Which U.S. state do you think is most likely to have glaciers? _____

4. A *compass* is a device with a needle that always points to the north. What is a compass rose? _____

5. The *equator* is an imaginary line around the middle of Earth. Does the equator go north and south or east and west? _____

6. What causes soil *erosion*? _____

7. Lines of *latitude* and *longitude* are imaginary lines that divide the earth into a grid. Which run north and south? _____ Run east and west? _____

8. A *volcano* is an opening in the earth's crust. Hot lava, ash, and gases are ejected from an active volcano. Name a U.S. state that has volcanoes. _____

ACTIVITY 94 **Use Reference Sources**
to Expand Knowledge

Name:_____

Date:_____

Select one of these topics. Use reference sources to learn more about the subject. Write a short report on another sheet of paper. Include drawings or copies of pictures.

*   How does a compass work?

*   Describe the climate at the equator and some plants and animals that live there.

*   Describe the causes of erosion and its effects on people, plants, and animals.

*   Explain why people use lines of latitude and longitude and how it helps them pinpoint locations on a map. Include information on degrees and minutes. Give the latitude and longitude for your city.

*   Describe a glacier and the effect it has on the land.

*   Write a general report about how and why volcanoes erupt. Include drawings and diagrams.

*   Write a report about a specific volcano in the United States.

ACTIVITY 95 Differentiate Between Facts and Opinions

Name:_____

Date:_____

Circle "F" for fact or "O" for opinion.

1.   F   O   A compass is the best tool to find your way to a place you haven't visited before.
2.   F   O   A compass is useless unless you want to go north.
3.   F   O   Exploring a glacier would be a great way to spend a vacation.
4.   F   O   Lines of latitude run parallel to the equator.
5.   F   O   Nobody cares about lines of longitude, so we shouldn't learn about them.
6.   F   O   It would really be interesting to climb down inside a volcano.
7.   F   O   Only a scientist would want to learn about volcanoes.
8.   F   O   Planting trees is one way to prevent erosion.
9.   F   O   Polar bears live only in the Northern Hemisphere.
10. F   O   Some Roman aqueducts are still in use today.
11. F   O   The equator is not necessary because it is an imaginary line.
12. F   O   The Mississippi River forms the boundary between Illinois and Iowa.
13. F   O   We should build more aqueducts.

ACTIVITY 96 Test-Taking

Name:_____

Date:_____

Write the letter of the answer that best matches the definition.

1. _____ an imaginary line around the middle of the earth, dividing it into two sections
   a. longitude   b. boundary   c. equator   d. hemisphere
2. _____ wearing away of something by rain, wind, or other processes
   a. eruption   b. erosion   c. volcano   d. glacier
3. _____ a place in the earth that ejects hot lava, ashes, and gas
   a. volcano   b. glacier   c. earthquake   d. equator
4. _____ a huge accumulation of ice, snow, water, rock, and sediment that moves slowly
   a. volcano   b. lava   c. tundra   d. glacier
5. _____ half of a sphere
   a. sphere   b. hemisphere c. equator   d. polar cap
6. _____ a tool that shows which way is north
   a. compass   b. atlas   c. map   d. protractor
7. _____ imaginary lines that run north and south on a globe or map
   a. compass   b. latitude   c. longitude   d. equator
8. _____ a channel built to carry water
   a. pipe   b. faucet   c. shower   d. aqueduct
9. _____ imaginary lines that run east and west on a globe or map
   a. boundary   b. latitude   c. longitude   d. hemisphere

ACTIVITY 97 Define Compound Words

Name:_____

Date:_____

A **compound word** combines two or more words to make a new word that expresses a single idea. Sometimes the meaning of the new word isn't clear even though you know the meaning of both words used.

All the words on this list include animal words, but none are the names of animals. Use a dictionary to help you answer the questions. Answer the questions on another sheet of paper.

1. For what would you use a *crowbar*?
2. Why would you *dog paddle* in a swimming pool?
3. If you need to run a long way, you might try going at a dogtrot. What is a *dogtrot*?
4. When people get involved in horseplay, sometimes someone gets hurt. What is *horseplay*?
5. You won't find a litterbug under a rock or building a web. What is a *litterbug*?
6. Monkeyshines are not apes that glow in the dark. What are *monkeyshines*?
7. A mare is a female horse or zebra. What is a *nightmare*?
8. People might put papers or other small items in a pigeonhole, but they wouldn't put a pigeon in one. What is a *pigeonhole*?
9. You might find a snapdragon in a flower garden. What is a *snapdragon*?
10. A sourpuss isn't a cat that ate a lemon. What is a *sourpuss*?

ACTIVITY 98 Match Compound Words With Illustrations

Name:_____

Date:_____

Write the word that matches each picture. Not all words will be used.

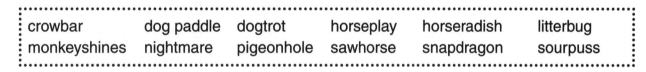

crowbar   dog paddle   dogtrot   horseplay   horseradish   litterbug
monkeyshines   nightmare   pigeonhole   sawhorse   snapdragon   sourpuss

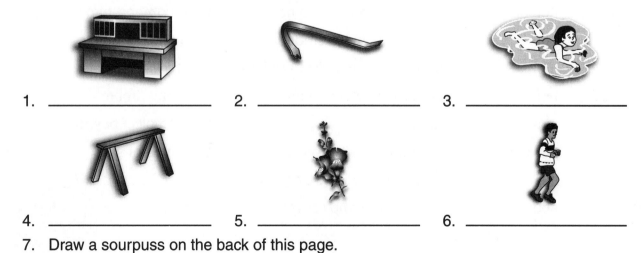

1. _____   2. _____   3. _____

4. _____   5. _____   6. _____

7. Draw a sourpuss on the back of this page.

ACTIVITY 99 Use Compound Words in Context

Name:_____

Date:_____

Write the word from the list that best fits with the meaning of the sentence.

| crowbar | dog paddle | dogtrot | horseplay | horseradish | litterbug |
| monkeyshines | nightmare | pigeonhole | sawhorse | snapdragon | sourpuss |

1. "Cheer up," Tori told Grandpa. "You look like a _____."
2. "No more _____!" Mom shouted. "It's time for bed."
3. _____ can get you in trouble if it gets too rough.
4. _____ sauce is good on roast beef sandwiches.
5. _____s come in red, yellow, and white.
6. A _____ doesn't respect public property.
7. Amy put the board on the _____ when she was ready to cut it.
8. Dan used a _____ to help roll the huge rock out of our way.
9. If you maintain a steady _____, it won't take long to run around the track.
10. Rhonda put the bills in a _____ until it was time to pay them.
11. Sometimes watching a scary show before bedtime can cause a _____.
12. When you _____, you keep your head out of the water. Your arms move forward when your legs move backwards.

ACTIVITY 100 Test-Taking

Name:_____

Date:_____

Write the letter of the answer that best matches the word.

1. _____ crowbar   a. place where crows sit   b. a pry bar or lever
2. _____ dog paddle   a. a swimming stroke   b. part of a boat
3. _____ dogtrot   a. a running dog   b. a steady jogging pace
4. _____ horseplay   a. to pretend to be a horse   b. rough-and-tumble play
5. _____ horseradish   a. a strongly flavored radish   b. a type of tomato
6. _____ monkeyshines   a. mischief, usually harmless   b. shiny apes
7. _____ nightmare   a. a dark-colored horse   b. a bad dream
8. _____ pigeonhole   a. a nest   b. a small cubbyhole
9. _____ sawhorse   a. a frame with legs, used to support wood being sawed   b. a type of saw
10. _____ sourpuss   a. a very grumpy person   b. a sad cat

ACTIVITY 101 **Define Transportation-** Name:_____

Related Words   Date:_____

Write the word from the list to match the definition. Use a dictionary if you are not sure of the meaning of a word.

> ambulance   automobile   aviation   cargo   carriage
> marine   helicopter   motorcycle   stagecoach   vehicle

1. a vehicle used to transport people to a hospital _____
2. a vehicle with a motor and four wheels used for personal travel _____
3. related to air travel _____
4. items carried by a vehicle from one place to another _____
5. a cart, wagon, or buggy pulled by an animal _____
6. related to water _____
7. a vehicle that can fly, hover, and ascend or descend in a straight line
   _____
8. a vehicle with a motor and two wheels _____
9. a vehicle for transporting people from stop to stop, pulled by horses _____
10. any manufactured device used for moving something from one place to another
    _____

ACTIVITY 102 **Critical Thinking**   Name:_____

                                               Date:_____

1. Cars and buses are two types of land vehicles. Name six other types of land vehicles.
   _____ _____ _____
   _____ _____ _____

2. *Cycle* means *wheel*. Why do you think *motor* and *cycle* were joined to describe this type of vehicle?
   _____

3. What other types of transportation use *cycle* as part of the word?
   _____ _____ _____

4. A vehicle is a manufactured device used for moving people or things from one place to another. Is a horse a vehicle? _____ Why or why not? _____
   _____

5. Is a covered wagon a vehicle? _____ Why or why not? _____
   _____

6. Why do you think people called cars horseless carriages when they were first invented?
   _____

7. Boats are vehicles used for transportation across water. Name three other types of marine transportation. _____ _____ _____

8. Helicopters are vehicles used for transportation by air. Name three other types of aviation vehicles.
   _____ _____ _____

ACTIVITY 103 Classify Vehicles/
Compare and Contrast

Name:_____

Date:_____

1. Write the words from the list that fit into each category. Add other words of your own.

airplane   ambulance   bicycle   rowboat   train   ship   canoe   taxi
go-cart   helicopter   kayak   raft   tractor   truck   blimp   motorcycle
submarine   hot air balloon

LAND TRANSPORTATION	AIR TRANSPORTATION	MARINE TRANSPORTATION

2. On another sheet of paper, compare and contrast any two vehicles on the list.

ACTIVITY 104 Test-Taking

Name:_____

Date:_____

Write the letter of the answer that best matches the definition.

1. _____   a vehicle pulled by horses to transport people and goods
            a. automobile   b. stagecoach   c.   helicopter   d. submarine
2. _____   a cart pulled by a horse or other animal
            a. kayak   b. taxi   c. carriage   d. truck
3. _____   related to air travel
            a. aviation   b. marine   c. submarine   d. pilot
4. _____   a motorized vehicle with two wheels
            a. motorcycle   b. bicycle   c. blimp   d. airplane
5. _____   a manufactured device used for transportation
            a. horse   b. roller skates   c. vehicle   d. jogging
6. _____   a vehicle used for personal transportation
            a. train   b. submarine   c. automobile   d. rocket
7. _____   a vehicle that can hover and fly
            a. airplane   b. stagecoach   c. helicopter   d. jet
8. _____   related to water
            a. marine   b. aviation   c. submarine   d. boat
9. _____   items carried by a vehicle from one place to another
            a. transportation   b. truck   c. train   d. cargo
10. _____   a vehicle for transporting people to a hospital
            a. airplane   b. ambulance   c. submarine   d. pickup truck

ACTIVITY 105　Define Words That Are Antonyms

Name:_____

Date:_____

Match the words with their definitions.

1. _____ ascend
2. _____ borrow
3. _____ descend
4. _____ export
5. _____ external
6. _____ factual
7. _____ fictional
8. _____ import
9. _____ internal
10. _____ loan
11. _____ maximum
12. _____ minimum

a. true
b. the least
c. to send products to another country
d. to rise
e. inside
f. to use, but promise to return
g. the most
h. not true, imaginary
i. outside
j. to give someone money or something to use for a time
k. to go down
l. to bring products in from another country

ACTIVITY 106　Recognize Antonyms/ Use Antonyms in Context

Name:_____

Date:_____

Antonyms are words that mean the opposite. *Example: Decrease* and *increase* are antonyms. Use the words from the list to write six sets of antonyms.

ascend	borrow	descend	export	external	factual
minimum	fictional	import	internal	loan	maximum

1. _____ and _____
2. _____ and _____
3. _____ and _____
4. _____ and _____
5. _____ and _____
6. _____ and _____

7. Give an example of something you could borrow. _____

8. Name a book or movie that is fictional. _____

9. Name a book or movie that is factual. _____

10. What is the minimum amount of cash you would need to buy a music CD? _____

11. When an elevator goes from the first to the second floor, does it ascend or descend?

_____

12. Is your heart an internal or external organ? _____

13. Check the labels to find something you own that was imported. What is it and where was it made? _____

ACTIVITY 107 Use Words in Context

Name:_____

Date:_____

Write the word from the list that best completes each sentence.

borrow	descend	export	external	factual
fictional	import	loan	maximum	minimum

1. Could I _____ your book? I left mine at home.
2. As the elevator began to _____ into the underground mine, it got harder to breathe.
3. What is the main _____ of the United States to China?
4. The long _____ antenna on the radio gave it more range.
5. Juan claimed his story was _____, but no one believed it really happened.
6. Hannah likes to read fables, tall tales, and other types of _____ stories.
7. Kyle knew his jacket was an _____ because the label said: Made in Germany.
8. Could you _____ me five dollars until tomorrow?
9. The skater tried her best by putting the _____ amount of effort into the race.
10. At the art auction, we learned that to begin, the _____ bid was $1,000.

ACTIVITY 108 Test-Taking

Name:_____

Date:_____

Write the letter of the answer that best defines each word.

1. _____ fictional   a. true   b. not true   c. books   d. movies
2. _____ descend   a. rise up   b. level   c. go down   d. stairs
3. _____ external   a. outside   b. interior   c. inside   d. far away
4. _____ import   a. important   b. bring in   c. buy   d. send out
5. _____ factual   a. fiction   b. books   c. movies   d. true
6. _____ maximum   a. the least   b. the most   c. money   d. some
7. _____ internal   a. heart   b. outside   c. rooms   d. inside
8. _____ export   a. send out   b. bring in   c. to carry   d. sell
9. _____ loan   a. to use   b. something given temporarily

                         c. money   d. a book
10. _____ ascend   a. ladder   b. go down   c. elevator   d. rise
11. _____ minimum   a. many   b. the most   c. a few   d. the least
12. _____ borrow   a. to use temporarily b. money   c. checks   d. cash

ACTIVITY 109 Write Synonyms for Review Words

Name: _____

Date: _____

Write a synonym for each word.

1. actual _____
2. ascend _____
3. boundary _____
4. descend _____
5. exact _____
6. external _____
7. formerly _____
8. hemisphere _____
9. instantly _____
10. keen _____
11. marine _____
12. minimum _____
13. nightmare _____
14. sourpuss _____
15. usual _____

16. annually _____
17. aviation _____
18. cargo _____
19. dog paddle _____
20. export _____
21. factual _____
22. gradually _____
23. import _____
24. internal _____
25. loan _____
26. maximum _____
27. naturally _____
28. regular _____
29. typical _____
30. usually _____

ACTIVITY 110 Match Review Words to Illustrations

Name: _____

Date: _____

1. _____

2. _____

3. _____

4. _____

5. _____

6. _____

7. _____

8. _____

Match each of the words below to an illustration. Then write each word on the correct line.
Review words: equator, compass rose, stagecoach, aqueduct, carriage, lines of latitude, volcano, lines of longitude

55

ACTIVITY 111 Define Adjectives

Name:_____

Date:_____

Adjectives are words that describe nouns.

> *Example:* The bear had long, shaggy, black hair.
>
> *Long, shaggy,* and *black* are adjectives that describe the hair.

Match the adjectives with their definitions. Use a dictionary if you are not sure of the meaning of a word.

1. _____ absolute
2. _____ adequate
3. _____ anxious
4. _____ drastic
5. _____ frigid
6. _____ immediate
7. _____ moderate
8. _____ obvious
9. _____ previous
10. _____ rapid

a. extreme; severe
b. reasonable; not too much or too little
c. worried
d. complete; total
e. clear
f. former; before now
g. enough
h. quick
i. direct; urgent
j. very cold

ACTIVITY 112 Write Nouns for Adjectives

Name:_____

Date:_____

Adjectives describe nouns.

In the following sentence, the adjectives are underlined. The nouns they describe are in bold print.
Example: The <u>frigid</u> **conditions** brought about an <u>immediate</u> **need** for <u>adequate</u> **shelter**.

Write two nouns (names of people, places, or things) that could be described by each adjective.

1. absolute _____ _____
2. adequate _____ _____
3. anxious _____ _____
4. drastic _____ _____
5. frigid _____ _____
6. immediate _____ _____
7. moderate _____ _____
8. obvious _____ _____
9. previous _____ _____
10. rapid _____ _____

ACTIVITY 113 Write Causes and Effects   Name:_____

Date:_____

Finish each sentence by writing a cause or an effect that makes sense.

1. The darkness was absolute, so Maria _____
    _____

2. Because there wasn't adequate heat in the building, _____
    _____

3. Because _____
    _____, June felt anxious.

4. Dana had to take drastic action because _____
    _____

5. There was only a moderate amount of milk left, so Brad _____
    _____

6. The source of the noise wasn't obvious, so Jake _____
    _____

7. He had failed on his previous try, so he _____
    _____

ACTIVITY 114 Test-Taking   Name:_____

Date:_____

Write the letter of the answer that best defines each word.

1. _____ absolute   a. total   b. most   c. some   d. none

2. _____ adequate   a. too much   b. enough   c. not enough   d. total

3. _____ anxious   a. enough   b. worried   c. angry   d. sad

4. _____ drastic   a. mild   b. quick   c. worried   d. extreme

5. _____ frigid   a. warm   b. cool   c. very cold   d. mild

6. _____ immediate   a. total   b. seldom   c. urgent   d. soon

7. _____ moderate   a. total   b. very little c. some   d. medium

8. _____ obvious   a. total   b. clear   c. likeable   d. unclear

9. _____ previous   a. earlier   b. later   c. urgent   d. soon

10. _____ rapid   a. moderate   b. slow   c. at once   d. quick

ACTIVITY 115 Define Adverbs

Name:_____

Date:_____

Adverbs are used with verbs, adjectives, or other adverbs to describe, limit, or make the meaning of the word clearer. Adding a suffix to a word changes the meaning of the word. Adding the suffix *-ly* to an adjective can change it to an adverb.

Example: Swift and *quick* are <u>adjectives</u>. *Swiftly* and *quickly* are <u>adverbs</u>.

Write the adjective form of each word. Then write a short definition for the adverb. Use a dictionary if you need help. The first one has been done as an example.

	Adjective	**Adverb**	**Definition of Adverb**
1.	*absolute*	absolutely	*totally*
2.	_____	adequately	_____
3.	_____	anxiously	_____
4.	_____	drastically	_____
5.	_____	frigidly	_____
6.	_____	immediately	_____
7.	_____	moderately	_____
8.	_____	obviously	_____

ACTIVITY 116 Differentiate Between Adjective and Adverb Forms

Name:_____

Date:_____

Circle the correct word in each sentence.

1. Jan (absolute / absolutely) refuses to wear a pink sweater.
2. Jay thinks ten hours is an (adequate / adequately) amount of sleep each night.
3. Rosa felt (anxious / anxiously) about winning the spelling bee.
4. She performed (adequate / adequately) in the competition.
5. Tasha knew she needed to take (drastic / drastically) action to save the baby bird.
6. The (frigid / frigidly) temperatures caused crops to freeze.
7. We have an (immediate / immediately) need for more help at the animal center.
8. Please come (immediate / immediately).
9. It is (obvious / obviously) that I will need a ladder to reach the ceiling.
10. (Obvious / Obviously), I cannot reach the ceiling without a ladder.
11. Zeke had visited the museum many times (previous / previously).
12. The (absolute / absolutely) darkness of the cave was frightening.
13. Andy (anxious / anxiously) waited for the results of the test.
14. The number of trees was (drastic / drastically) reduced after the forest fire.

ACTIVITY 117 Use Words in Context/ Journal Writing

Name: _____

Date: _____

Write a journal entry about an imaginary visit to the North Pole in winter. Use five or more words from the list. Use another sheet of paper if you need more room.

absolutely	adequately	anxiously	drastically	frigidly
immediately	moderately	obviously	previously	rapidly

_____

_____

_____

_____

_____

_____

_____

_____

ACTIVITY 118 Test-Taking

Name: _____

Date: _____

Write the letter of the answer that best defines each adverb.

1. _____ moderately   a. totally   b. quickly   c. seldom   d. fairly
2. _____ rapidly   a. moderately   b. quickly   c. at once   d. slowly
3. _____ adequately   a. mostly   b. satisfactorily c. rarely   d. totally
4. _____ anxiously   a. happily   b. worriedly   c. angrily   d. sadly
5. _____ absolutely   a. totally   b. mostly   c. partly   d. none
6. _____ drastically   a. mildly   b. partly   c. quickly   d. extremely
7. _____ immediately   a. totally   b. seldom   c. urgently   d. slowly
8. _____ obviously   a. totally   b. clearly   c. slowly   d. partly
9. _____ frigidly   a. warmly   b. coolly   c. coldly   d. mildly
10. _____ previously   a. after   b. later   c. urgently   d. before

ACTIVITY 119   Define Noun Forms of Verbs

Name:_____

Date:_____

Adding a suffix to the end of a word changes the meaning of the word. The suffix *-tion* changes verbs to nouns. When a word ends in *t*, add only *-ion*.

Use a dictionary to answer the questions if you are unsure of a word.

1. To *attract* means to catch someone's attention. What is an *attraction*?

    _____

2. To *collect* means to gather things or money. What is a *collection*?

    _____

3. To *construct* means to build. What is a *construction*?

    _____

4. To *infect* means to pass a disease to another person. What is an *infection*?

    _____

5. To *instruct* means to teach. What does *instruction* mean?

    _____

6. To *protect* means to guard or defend. What does *protection* mean?

    _____

ACTIVITY 120   Relate Vocabulary Words to Daily Life

Name:_____

Date:_____

Answer the following questions on another sheet of paper.
1. What color bird is most likely to attract your attention?
2. What color hair do you think is the most attractive?
3. Name an attraction you have visited. (It could be something famous like the Statue of Liberty or a local place such as a historic building.) Briefly describe your reaction to the attraction.
4. Have you ever helped collect money or other items for a charity? Describe what you helped collect and why.
5. A dam built by beavers, a nest, and a beehive are types of constructions built by animals. Name another type of construction built by an animal.
6. Name something you have helped to construct. (It could be something made of wood, blocks, or a model.)
7. Have you ever had an infection? What did you do to get better?
8. People take instruction outside of school in many things, such as art, music, or dance. Name five specific types of instruction.
9. Many items that we use daily help to protect us. An umbrella protects us from rain. Shoes protect our feet from cuts. Name five other things that provide protection.
10. Do you have any collections? What do you collect?

ACTIVITY 121   Use Words in Context

Name:_____

Date:_____

Write words from the list to complete the sentences. Not all words will be used.

attract	attraction	collect	collection	construct	construction
infect	infection	instruct	instruction	protect	protection

1. A smile is one of the best ways to _____ friends.
2. Aaron builds houses. He works in _____.
3. He can _____ almost anything from wood.
4. Gina asked the coach to _____ her on how to become a better tennis player.
5. If we _____ aluminum cans, we turn them in for money at the recycling center.
6. Leslie's favorite _____ at the museum is the T-rex skeleton.
7. Most projects go more smoothly if you read the _____ first.
8. Stay away from Grant. He has a bad cold and could _____ you.
9. The doctor gave Kyle pills because he had an ear _____.
10. The light jacket Terri wore provided little _____ against the cold.

ACTIVITY 122   Test-Taking

Name:_____

Date:_____

Circle "T" for true or "F" for false.

1. T F   A **collection** is a group of things, such as stamps or baseball cards.
2. T F   To **instruct** means to learn something new.
3. T F   If ants get in your house, it is called an **infection**.
4. T F   To **protect** means to use an umbrella.
5. T F   If someone **infects** you, you will get sick.
6. T F   **Instructions** can be written or drawn.
7. T F   Only people can make **constructions**.
8. T F   A haunted house is a type of **attraction**.
9. T F   To **collect** means to scatter things around.
10. T F   **Protection** is something that helps keep you safe.
11. T F   To **construct** means to build.
12. T F   When you **attract** people's attention, you try to hide from them.

ACTIVITY 123 Recognize and Write Compound Words

Name:_____

Date:_____

A **compound word** combines two or more words to make a new word that expresses a single idea. *Toadstool, blueberry,* and *keyboard* are compound words.

1. Draw a line to separate the two words used to make each compound word.

    a. backup   b. groundskeeper   c. livestock   d. overcome

    e. overdo   f. overdue   g. overshoes   h. overturn

    i. stockroom j. stockyard   k. turnover   l. wetsuit

2. Combine another word with each word below to make a compound word.

    back_____   up_____   shoe_____

    yard_____   suit_____   room_____

    _____room   _____up   _____back

ACTIVITY 124 Define Compound Words

Name:_____

Date:_____

Sometimes you can learn the meaning of a compound word by looking at the words used. Sometimes the meaning of the new word isn't clear, even though you know the meaning of both words used.

Use another sheet of paper to answer these questions. Use a dictionary if you need help.

1. To *back up* means to drive in reverse. What does it mean to make a *backup* of something?
2. A *groundskeeper* takes care of an outside area such as a park, lawn, or golf course. What types of jobs would a groundskeeper do?
3. To *overcome* means to conquer or to win. Use *overcome* in a sentence.
4. To *overdo* does not mean the same as to *do over*. What does *overdo* mean?
5. Overdue and overdo sound the same, but have different meanings. What does *overdue* mean?
6. Overshoes are boots worn over shoes to keep your shoes dry in rain or snow. Why do you think the words *over* and *shoes* were combined for this meaning?
7. *Overturn* and *turnover* combine the same two words, but they have different meanings. What does *overturn* mean?
8. A *turnover* is a type of dessert. Describe a turnover.
9. *Stock* can mean supplies or items sold in a store. What is a *stockroom*?
10. *Stock* is also another word used for cattle and other animals raised on a farm. They are often called *livestock*. What is a *stockyard*?

ACTIVITY 125 Use Compound Words in Context

Name:_____

Date:_____

It is necessary to know when to use a compound word and when to use the two words separately. You can do this by carefully reading the sentence. Circle the correct word or words in each sentence.

1. I forgot my hairbrush, so I had to go (back up / backup) the stairs to get it.
2. Can you help the (grounds keeper / groundskeeper) tend the flowerbeds?
3. Until the storm is (over, come / overcome) inside and wait.
4. The storm is almost (over, do / overdo) nothing else for now.
5. Our flight was (over due / overdue).
6. What a mess! I spilled paint (over shoes / overshoes) and socks.
7. "Since the excitement is (over, turn / overturn) around and go back to class," said the teacher.
8. The farmer took his (live stock / livestock) to the fair.
9. If we (stock rooms / stockrooms) in our house with these large crates, we will not have much room to move.
10. The (stock, yards, / stockyards) and fences were covered with snow.
11. Don't forget to (turn over / turnover) the pancakes before they burn.

ACTIVITY 126 Test-Taking

Name:_____

Date:_____

Circle "T" for true or "F" for false.

1. T F To **backup** means to make a copy.
2. T F A **groundskeeper** is a person in charge of coffee grounds.
3. T F To **overcome** means the same as to come over.
4. T F **Overdo** means late.
5. T F Most libraries charge a fee if books are **overdue.**
6. T F No one ever wears **overshoes** anymore.
7. T F To **overturn** something means to turn over a new leaf, or make a change.
8. T F **Livestock** is another word for animals raised on a farm or a ranch.
9. T F A **stockroom** is a room where socks are kept.
10. T F A **stockyard** is a place where chickens are kept.
11. T F A **turnover** is a type of dessert.
12. T F People who go scuba diving wear a **wetsuit.**

ACTIVITY 127　Define Scientific Words

Name: _____

Date: _____

Use a dictionary to help you with the answers.

1. The word *biology* comes from two Greek words, *bio*, meaning life, and *logia*, to study. What does *biology* mean? _____
2. One branch of biology is *botany*. Botany is the study of _____.
3. Another branch of biology is *zoology*. What is zoology? _____
4. *Chemistry* is the science of _____.
5. The Greek word for earth is *geo*. What is geology? _____
6. *Solar* comes from the Latin word *sol*, meaning sun. What does solar mean?

   _____
7. *Lunar* comes from a Latin word for moon. What does *lunar* mean?

   _____
8. *Stellar* comes from a Latin word meaning star. What does *stellar* mean?

   _____

9. A person who is skilled in math is called a _____.
10. A person who studies history is called a _____.

ACTIVITY 128　Define Related Words

Name: _____

Date: _____

Adding a suffix to the end of a word changes the meaning of the word. Sometimes the spelling of the root word changes. The suffix *-ist* means <u>one who studies</u>. Use a dictionary if you are not sure of an answer or need to check the spelling of a word.

1. A _____ is a person who studies life.
2. A _____ is a person who studies plants.
3. A _____ is a person who studies the earth.
4. A _____ is a person who studies science.
5. A _____ is a person who studies animals.

6. What does *solar power* mean? _____
7. Which of these subjects do you think is the most interesting: biology, botany, mathematics, history, zoology, or chemistry? _____
8. Why? _____

   _____
9. Would you like to take a lunar voyage? _____ Why or why not? _____

   _____
10. *Stellar* means related to the stars. It also means outstanding. Why do you think the word *stellar* also means outstanding? _____

    _____

ACTIVITY 129   Use Words in Context

Name:_____

Date:_____

Write words from the list to complete the sentences. Not all words will be used.

biologist	biology	botanist	botany	chemist	chemistry
geologist	geology	historian	lunar	mathematician	
scientist	solar	stellar	zoologist	zoology	

1. _____ is the study of the origin, history, and structure of the earth.
2. A cartographer is a mapmaker. A _____ cartographer maps the stars.
3. Some people use _____ power to heat their homes.
4. Astronauts made the first _____ landing in 1969.
5. _____ and botany are two branches of _____.
6. A _____ would be very interested in studying a new type of animal.
7. We found a weird rock in a cave, so we took it to a _____ to be identified.
8. Kiko enjoys working with plants. She plans to study _____ in college.
9. Botany Bay in Australia was named by a _____ because of the wide variety of exotic plants he found on its shores.
10. A _____ works with many chemicals.
11. Pam called a local _____ to learn more about the 200-year-old house they bought.

ACTIVITY 130   Test-Taking

Name:_____

Date:_____

Circle "T" for true or "F" for false.

1. T   F   A **botanist** studies trees and other plants.
2. T   F   A **geologist** would be a good person to ask about how trees grow.
3. T   F   **Chemistry** is the study of people with unusual diseases.
4. T   F   A **biologist** studies volcanoes and earthquakes.
5. T   F   **Geology** includes the study of rocks and minerals.
6. T   F   If you want to learn about current events, you should ask a **historian**.
7. T   F   A **chemist** is a type of scientist.
8. T   F   **Solar** power uses energy from the sun.
9. T   F   A **stellar** voyage means a trip to Australia.
10. T   F   A **zoologist** can only work in a zoo.
11. T   F   **Geology** and history are branches of **biology**.
12. T   F   A **chemist** would be the best person to call if you discovered a new type of butterfly.
13. T   F   **Zoology** is the study of animals.
14. T   F   A **mathematician** is a person who is not very good at math.

ACTIVITY 131 Use Definitions of Nouns to Write Sentences

Name:_____

Date:_____

Nouns are words that name people, places, things, or ideas. All of the words on this list are nouns. Read the definition of each noun. Write a sentence on another sheet of paper using the word correctly.

1. **apology:** a request for forgiveness
2. **delivery:** a shipment or package received
3. **deputy:** a person second in command to a sheriff
4. **discovery:** something new that is found
5. **melody:** a song or tune
6. **penalty:** a fine or punishment for an offense
7. **property:** something that belongs to someone
8. **quantity:** the number or amount of something
9. **technology:** an invention or change in machines or procedures
10. **variety:** a number of similar, but different, things

ACTIVITY 132 Write Plurals of Nouns Ending in "y"

Name:_____

Date:_____

Singular means one. **Plural** means more than one. To write the plural of most nouns, add an *s*. If a noun ends in a consonant and a *y*, change the *y* to *i* and add *-es*. (Do not change the *y* to *i* if a vowel comes before the *y*.)

Examples: history – histories; secretary – secretaries; monkey – monkeys

Write the plural form of the noun from the list to complete each sentence. Use a dictionary if you wish to check the spelling of a word.

| apology | delivery | deputy | discovery | melody |
| penalty | property | quantity | technology | variety |

1. When hockey players are given _____, they must sit in a box for a while.
2. Many important _____ have been made by accident.
3. Rosa grew many _____ of lilies in her garden.
4. Steve was sorry for his actions and made _____ to everyone in his class.
5. The introduction of new _____ in the last ten years has changed the way in which we live.
6. The landlord owned many _____ on the east side of town.
7. The numbers 139 and 422 represent _____ higher than 100.
8. The three _____ worked with the sheriff to solve the crime.
9. We are expecting several _____ of new books in the next few days.
10. Sean learned to play four new _____ on his bagpipe.

ACTIVITY 133 Use Words in Context/ Write Headlines

Name:_____

Date:_____

Use the singular or plural of each word to write an imaginary headline for a news story. Headlines should be six words or less.

1. apology   _____

2. delivery   _____

3. deputy   _____

4. discovery   _____

5. melody   _____

6. penalty   _____

7. property   _____

8. quantity   _____

9. technology _____

10. variety   _____

ACTIVITY 134 Test-Taking

Name:_____

Date:_____

Write the letter of the answer that best replaces the **** in each sentence.

1. _____ Sean made a(n) ****, but the coach would not accept it.
   a. apology   b. apologies   c. discovery   d. discoveries

2. _____ The DVD store made a special **** when my order arrived.
   a. deliveries   b. delivery   c. discovery   d. discoveries

3. _____ **** Watson arrested Sean for disturbing the peace.
   a. Deputy   b. Deputies   c. Penalty   d. Penalties

4. _____ Su made many important **** during her years as a scientist.
   a. discovery   b. discoveries   c. delivery   d. deliveries

5. _____ Sarah played several **** she had learned on the tuba.
   a. quantity   b. quantities   c. melody   d. melodies

6. _____ If you do not return your DVDs on time, you must pay a(n) ****.
   a. apology   b. apologies   c. penalty   d. penalties

7. _____ The city owned many ****, which they turned into playgrounds and parks.
   a. property   b. properties   c. variety   d. varieties

8. _____ I need a large **** of nails to fix my roof.
   a. quantity   b. quantities   c. technology   d. technologies

9. _____ Our computer includes the latest ****.
   a. discovery   b. discoveries   c. technology   d. technologies

10. _____ A sapsucker is one of many **** of woodpecker.
    a. quantity   b. quantities   c. variety   d. varieties

ACTIVITY 135 Write Synonyms for Review Words

Name: _____

Date: _____

Write a synonym for each word.

1. _____ absolutely
2. _____ attract
3. _____ collect
4. _____ construction
5. _____ frigid
6. _____ instruction
7. _____ lunar
8. _____ overdue
9. _____ previously
10. _____ protect
11. _____ quantity
12. _____ solar

13. _____ adequate
14. _____ backup
15. _____ construct
16. _____ delivery
17. _____ immediately
18. _____ livestock
19. _____ melody
20. _____ penalty
21. _____ property
22. _____ protection
23. _____ rapid
24. _____ stellar

ACTIVITY 136 Use Adjectives in Context

Name: _____

Date: _____

Write five sentences. Use at least three of the words from the list as adjectives in each sentence. Underline the words from the list.

absolute	adequate	anxious	backup	biology	chemistry
drastic	frigid	geology	immediate	lunar	moderate
obvious	previous	property	quantity	solar	stellar

1. _____

_____

2. _____

_____

3. _____

_____

4. _____

_____

5. _____

_____

ACTIVITY 137 · Write Compound Words

Name:_____

Date:_____

Combine words from the list to make 15 or more compound words. Words can be used to make more than one compound word.

back	case	come	do	due	grounds	wet	yard	turn
keeper	live	over	room	shoes	stairs	stock	suit	up

_____   _____   _____

_____   _____   _____

_____   _____   _____

_____   _____   _____

_____   _____

_____   _____

_____   _____

_____   _____

_____   _____

ACTIVITY 138 · Classify Words

Name:_____

Date:_____

A **noun** names a person, place, thing, or idea. Write "N" if the word is a noun. A **verb** is an action word. Write "V" if the word is a verb. An **adjective** describes a noun. Write "ADJ" if the word is an adjective. An **adverb** answers the questions *when, how, why, how much, how often,* and *to what extent.* Write "ADV" if the word is an adverb.

1. _____ absolute
2. _____ overturn
3. _____ absolutely
4. _____ apology
5. _____ solar
6. _____ biologist
7. _____ delivery
8. _____ drastic
9. _____ scientist
10. _____ immediate
11. _____ instruction
12. _____ melody

13. _____ adequate
14. _____ penalty
15. _____ historian
16. _____ adequately
17. _____ stellar
18. _____ chemist
19. _____ deputy
20. _____ frigidly
21. _____ lunar
22. _____ infection
23. _____ livestock
24. _____ moderately

25. _____ anxious
26. _____ previously
27. _____ anxiously
28. _____ chemistry
29. _____ collect
30. _____ discovery
31. _____ zoologist
32. _____ geologist
33. _____ stockyard
34. _____ instruct
35. _____ mathematician
36. _____ obviously

ACTIVITY 139 Match Animal Words With Illustrations

Name:_____

Date:_____

Write the names of the animals below their pictures. Use a dictionary or other reference source if you are not sure of your answers. Not all words will be used.

| cottonmouth | hedgehog | jellyfish | polecat | rattlesnake |
| sailfish | sapsucker | turtledove | wolfhound | roadrunner |

1. _____ 2. _____ 3. _____ 4. _____

5. _____ 6. _____ 7. _____ 8. _____

ACTIVITY 140 Classify Animals

Name:_____

Date:_____

Write words from the list for each group. Some words may be used more than once. Use a dictionary if you are not sure of an animal. Add other animal names not on the list for each group.

cottonmouth

hedgehog

jellyfish

polecat

rattlesnake

roadrunner

sailfish

sapsucker

silkworm

silverfish

turtledove

wolfhound

SNAKES	MAMMALS	BIRDS
INSECTS	**LAND ANIMALS**	**SEA ANIMALS**

ACTIVITY 141 Creative Thinking

Name:_____

Date:_____

Make up a silly definition for each compound word based on the two words used to name the animal. *Example:* A hummingbird could be a bird that doesn't know the words to a song. Use another sheet of paper if you need more room.

1. cottonmouth _____
2. hedgehog _____
3. jellyfish _____
4. polecat _____
5. rattlesnake _____
6. roadrunner _____
7. sailfish _____
8. sapsucker _____
9. silkworm _____
10. silverfish _____
11. turtledove _____
12. wolfhound _____

ACTIVITY 142 Test-Taking

Name:_____

Date:_____

Write the letter of the answer that best matches the definition.

1. _____ This bird is a type of woodpecker that feeds on insects and tree sap.
    a. roadrunner　　b. robin　　　　c. ostrich　　　d. sapsucker
2. _____ Not a fish, this animal lives in salt water and has poisonous tentacles.
    a. seahorse　　　b. jellyfish　　c. squid　　　　d. octopus
3. _____ This small spiny mammal is often kept as a pet.
    a. hedgehog　　　b. porcupine　　c. jellyfish　　d. opossum
4. _____ Although it can fly, this bird can usually be seen racing across land.
    a. turtledove　　b. roadrunner　　c. penguin　　d. ostrich
5. _____ This member of the weasel family emits a disagreeable odor like a skunk when scared.
    a. bobcat　　　　b. raccoon　　　c. polecat　　　d. wombat
6. _____ This insect is the larva form of a moth.
    a. angleworm　　b. silverfish　　c. sailfish　　　d. silkworm
7. _____ This wingless insect is a common household pest.
    a. Goliath beetle　b. silkworm　　c. silverfish　　d. roadrunner
8. _____ Also called a water moccasin; the inside of this poisonous snake's mouth is white.
    a. rattlesnake　　b. cottonmouth　c. pit viper　　d. cobra
9. _____ This bird is a type of pigeon.
    a. sparrow　　　　b. roadrunner　　c. turtledove　　d. sapsucker
10. _____ This dog was originally a Russian hunting dog.
    a. sheep dog　　　b. poodle　　　c. beagle　　　d. wolfhound

　　　　　71

ACTIVITY 143 Define Words That Are Nouns

Name:_____

Date:_____

Match the words with their definitions. Use a dictionary if you are not sure of the meaning of a word.

1. _____ comparison
2. _____ conclusion
3. _____ consideration
4. _____ convention
5. _____ delegation
6. _____ denial
7. _____ ignorance
8. _____ legislature
9. _____ production
10. _____ provisions
11. _____ representative
12. _____ situation

a. rejection
b. a group who represents others
c. a person who represents others
d. ending
e. a group responsible for making laws
f. supplies
g. a meeting; a conference
h. manufacturing; making goods
i. condition; state of affairs
j. lack of knowledge
k. kindness
l. a statement of similarities and differences

WELCOME
TO THE
ANNUAL
INVENTION
CONVENTION

ACTIVITY 144 Use Words in Context

Name:_____

Date:_____

Write words from the list to complete the sentences. Not all words will be used.

| comparison | conclusion | consideration | convention | delegation | denial |
| ignorance | legislature | production | provisions | representative | situation |

1. For a science project, Ellen did a _____ of twelve types of toothpaste.
2. Her _____ was that none of them worked better than simply brushing with baking soda.
3. She presented her findings at the state science _____.
4. Ellen was part of the _____ from our school.
5. A _____ from one toothpaste company refused to accept her results.
6. He voiced a strong _____ of her experiment and made _____ to rerun the tests.
7. He also claimed that the _____ of toothpaste was based on a formula developed by dentists.
8. So far, the _____ has not been resolved.

ACTIVITY 145 Determine and Define Root Words

Name:_____

Date:_____

For each noun, write the verb form with a short definition. Use a dictionary if you are unsure of the verb, its spelling, or definition. The first one has been done as an example.

	NOUN	VERB	DEFINITION
1.	comparison	*compare*	*to look for ways things are alike or different*
2.	conclusion		
3.	consideration		
4.	convention		
5.	delegation		
6.	denial		
7.	ignorance		
8.	legislature		
9.	production		
10.	provisions		
11.	representative		
12.	situation		

ACTIVITY 146 Test-Taking

Name:_____

Date:_____

Write the letter of the answer that is the best definition for each word.

1. _____ comparison
   - a. condition
   - b. differences
   - c. similarities and differences
   - d. results

2. _____ conclusion
   - a. ending
   - b. first
   - c. decision
   - d. a coma

3. _____ consideration
   - a. think
   - b. happiness
   - c. kindness
   - d. feeling

4. _____ convention
   - a. group of people
   - b. science fair
   - c. circus
   - d. a meeting

5. _____ delegation
   - a. a group who represents others
   - b. people
   - c. one who agrees
   - d. toothpaste

6. _____ denial
   - a. agreement
   - b. respect
   - c. rejection
   - d. daily

7. _____ ignorance
   - a. lack of knowledge
   - b. smart
   - c. lack of sleep
   - d. tired

8. _____ legislature
   - a. people
   - b. Washington
   - c. a group who makes laws
   - d. the president

9. _____ production
   - a. reduction
   - b. factory
   - c. workers
   - d. manufacturing

10. _____ provisions
    - a. food
    - b. supplies
    - c. money
    - d. medicines

ACTIVITY 147 Define Words That Are Verbs

Name:_____

Date:_____

Verbs are action words. All of the words on this list are verbs. Write the word from the list to match its definition. Use a dictionary if you are not sure of the meaning of a word.

combine	compete	concentrate	contribute	demonstrate	detain
examine	explain	inform	locate	prevent	refrigerate

1. _____ to stop someone or something
2. _____ to donate something, such as time, money, or goods
3. _____ to join two or more things together
4. _____ to give details or make something clear
5. _____ to find
6. _____ to put something in a place to keep it cool
7. _____ to think hard on one subject
8. _____ to hold back
9. _____ to test; to look at very closely
10. _____ to show
11. _____ to try to do better than someone else at a sport or a task
12. _____ to tell

ACTIVITY 148 Use Words in Context

Name:_____

Date:_____

Write words from the list to complete the sentences. Not all words will be used.

combine	compete	concentrate	contribute	demonstrate	detain
examine	explain	inform	locate	prevent	refrigerate

1. A microscope helps you _____ small items closely.
2. I can stay for a minute, but do not _____ me too long, or I will miss my bus.
3. Didn't anyone ever _____ to you why you shouldn't play with matches?
4. If you do not _____ milk, it will get sour.
5. People often _____ peanut butter and jelly to make a sandwich.
6. Some people find it hard to _____ on schoolwork when the TV is on.
7. Volunteers who are willing to _____ their time are always welcome.
8. Will you _____ how to program my new DVD player?
9. Will you _____ the coach that today's game has been cancelled?
10. Would you like to _____ in a marathon? It is a 26-mile race.

ACTIVITY 149 Use Words in Context/ Write an Imaginary Recipe

Name:_____

Date:_____

Write a letter or e-mail to a friend telling about a new totally weird recipe you have just created. Use at least six of the words from the list. For example, you could tell how you came up with the idea for fried shoelaces with pumpkin sauce or CDs boiled in toothpaste juice.

combine	compete	concentrate	contribute	demonstrate	detain
examine	explain	inform	locate	prevent	refrigerate

_____

_____

_____

_____

_____

_____

_____

_____

_____

ACTIVITY 150 Test-Taking

Name:_____

Date:_____

Write "A" if the words are antonyms or "S" if the words are synonyms.

1. _____ combine and join
2. _____ concentrate and think
3. _____ demonstrate and show
4. _____ dream and concentrate
5. _____ explain and question
6. _____ inform and ask
7. _____ lose and locate
8. _____ refrigerate and cool
9. _____ start and prevent
10. _____ take and contribute

11. _____ compete and cooperate
12. _____ contribute and give
13. _____ detain and hold
14. _____ experiment and test
15. _____ free and detain
16. _____ locate and find
17. _____ prevent and stop
18. _____ separate and combine
19. _____ study and examine
20. _____ warm and refrigerate

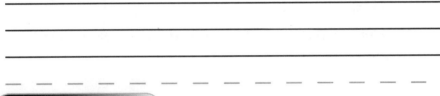

ACTIVITY 151 Define Nouns Derived From Verbs

Name:_____

Date:_____

Match the words to their definitions.

1. _____ combination
2. _____ competition
3. _____ concentration
4. _____ contribution
5. _____ demonstration
6. _____ detention
7. _____ examination
8. _____ explanation
9. _____ information
10. _____ location
11. _____ prevention
12. _____ refrigeration

a. attention
b. a visual display
c. the act of cooling
d. a place
e. a statement that makes something easy to understand
f. a contest
g. a donation
h. facts needed to make a decision
i. a mixture
j. the act of stopping
k. a test
l. a form of punishment; a place where someone is kept for a time

ACTIVITY 152 Determine Root Words/ Use Words in Context

Name:_____

Date:_____

When a suffix is added to a word, it changes the meaning of the word. It may also change the spelling of the root word. Adding the suffixes *-ion*, *-tion*, or *-ation* changes verbs to nouns.

Write the verb form for each noun. Use a dictionary if you are not sure of the spelling of the verb.

NOUN	VERB		NOUN	VERB
1. combination	_____		8. contribution	_____
2. concentration	_____		9. detention	_____
3. demonstration	_____		10. explanation	_____
4. examination	_____		11. location	_____
5. information	_____		12. refrigeration	_____
6. prevention	_____			
7. competition	_____			

Select any five of the above nouns, and then on another sheet of paper, write a sentence for each noun.

ACTIVITY 153 Use Words in Context

Name: _____

Date: _____

Write words from the list to complete the sentences.
Not all words will be used.

combination	competition	concentration	contribution	demonstration	detention
examination	explanation	information	location	prevention	refrigeration

1. Angie needed more _____ to decide which computer to buy.

2. Before people had _____, food spoiled much quicker.

3. No one has yet found the _____ of the pot of gold at the end of the rainbow.

4. Not everyone who enters a _____ can be the winner.

5. Roger had _____ for a week after the food fight in the cafeteria.

6. The _____ of raisins, nuts, sunflower seeds, chow mein noodles, and
    mints makes a tasty snack.

7. The animal shelter is asking for _____s of dog and cat food.

8. The scientist noticed a high _____ of iron in the rock.

9. To prepare for an _____, study hard and get lots of sleep.

10. Would you rather read about how to do something or watch a _____?

ACTIVITY 154 Test-Taking

Name: _____

Date: _____

Write the letter of the answer that
is the best synonym for each word.

1. _____ mixture   a. recipe   b. combination   c. combine

2. _____ contest   a. compete   b. competition   c. test

3. _____ focus   a. see   b. look   c. concentration

4. _____ donation   a. contribute   b. contribution   c. money

5. _____ visual display   a. demonstration   b. show   c. demonstrate

6. _____ punishment   a. detention   b. detain   c. exam

7. _____ test   a. learn   b. teach   c. examination

8. _____ details   a. explanation   b. question   c. explain

9. _____ knowledge   a. school   b. information   c. inform

10. _____ place   a. prevention   b. rest   c. location

11. _____ obstacle   a. prevention   b. prevent   c. course

12. _____ cooling   a. air   b. refrigeration   c. fan

ACTIVITY 155   Define Confusing Words

Name:_____

Date:_____

Write the word from the list to match the definitions. Use a dictionary if you are not sure of the meaning of a word.

> capital   capitol   coma   comma   desert   dessert
> irrigate   irritate   liter   litter   sympathy   symphony

1. a building where members of state or national government meet _____
2. a city that is the official seat of government of a state or nation _____
3. a feeling or expression of sorrow for the distress of another _____
4. a metric unit of measurement _____
5. a punctuation mark that looks like this: , _____
6. a state of deep unconsciousness, usually as a result of injury or disease _____
7. garbage left in public places; offspring of a mammal _____
8. a sweet treat often eaten after a meal _____
9. an area that receives very little rain _____
10. music for an orchestra _____
11. to bother someone _____
12. to water a garden, lawn, or field _____

- -

ACTIVITY 156   Use Words in Context

Name:_____

Date:_____

Circle the correct word in each sentence.

1. After six weeks without rain, it was necessary to (irrigate / irritate) the cornfield.
2. After the accident, Sharon was in a (coma / comma) for three weeks.
3. Is Portland the (capital / capitol) of Maine or Oregon?
4. Many types of plants and animals live in a (desert / dessert).
5. Please accept our (sympathy / symphony) on your loss.
6. Please turn the music down or it will (irrigate / irritate) the neighbors.
7. Soda often comes in a two- (liter / litter) bottle.
8. The senators met at the (capital / capitol) building to discuss the proposed law.
9. The squirrel had a (liter / litter) of four babies.
10. Use a (coma / comma) after the greeting in a friendly letter.
11. Would you like cake or pie for (desert / dessert)?
12. Would you like to go with me to hear the (sympathy / symphony) on Saturday?

ACTIVITY 157 Determine Facts or Opinions

Name:_____

Date:_____

Circle "F" for fact or "O" for opinion.

1.   F   O   A **liter** is less than a gallon.

2.   F   O   A **litter** of kittens is a beautiful sight.

3.   F   O   A person in a **coma** cannot move his or her body.

4.   F   O   A **symphony** orchestra is better to listen to than a jazz band.

5.   F   O   Bagpipe music is **irritating**.

6.   F   O   **Capital** letters are easier to write than lowercase letters.

7.   F   O   Farmers need to **irrigate** crops during dry weather so they grow.

8.   F   O   Ice cream is the best **dessert**.

9.   F   O   Rattlesnakes and cactus live in the **desert**.

10. F   O   You express your **sympathy** when someone dies.

11. F   O   The **Capitol** building in Washington, D.C., is a beautiful building.

12. F   O   Use **commas** to separate words in a series.

ACTIVITY 158 Test-Taking

Name:_____

Date:_____

Write the letter of the answer that best matches the definition.

1. _____ a city that is the official seat of government
   a. comma   b. capitol   c. capital   d. coma

2. _____ a feeling or expression of sorrow for another
   a. irritate   b. symphony   c. irrigate   d. sympathy

3. _____ a metric unit of measurement
   a. liter   b. desert   c. litter   d. dessert

4. _____ a sweet treat often eaten after a meal
   a. capital   b. dessert   c. desert   d. capitol

5. _____ a punctuation mark that looks like this: ,
   a. comma   b. period   c. coma   d. question mark

6. _____ an area that receives very little rain
   a. plain   b. plane   c. desert   d. dessert

7. _____ music for an orchestra
   a. sympathy   b. melody   c. musicians   d. symphony

8. _____ a state of deep unconsciousness
   a. capital   b. comma   c. coma   d. capitol

9. _____ garbage left in public places; offspring of a mammal
   a. litter   b. capitol   c. capital   d. liter

10. _____ to bother someone
    a. sympathy   b. irritate   c. irrigate   d. symphony

79

ACTIVITY 159 Define Compound Words

Name:_____

Date:_____

A **compound word** combines two or more words to make a new word that expresses a single idea. *Hardheaded, underhanded,* and *thumbtack* are compound words.

Each of the compound words on this list includes a word that refers to a part of the body. All of the words have a meaning that is much different from either of the words used to make the compound word. Match the words with their definitions. Use a dictionary if you are unsure of the meaning of a word.

1. _____ brainstorm
2. _____ bullheaded
3. _____ butterfingers
4. _____ footloose
5. _____ headfirst
6. _____ headline
7. _____ headway
8. _____ high-handed
9. _____ tenderhearted
10. _____ tightfisted
11. _____ tight-lipped
12. _____ underhanded

a. title of an article
b. hasty; impulsive; rash
c. kind
d. to search for ideas to solve a problem
e. free to do as one pleases
f. sneaky
g. miserly; stingy
h. clumsy
i. progress
j. silent; secretive
k. bossy
l. stubborn

ACTIVITY 160 Use Words in Context

Name:_____

Date:_____

Finish each sentence in your own words.

1. The students brainstormed for ideas on how to improve _____.
2. Eric turned bullheaded when his sister told him to _____.
3. When Suzanne dropped the _____, the coach knew she had butterfingers.
4. Because Angelo was footloose on Saturday, he decided to _____.
5. Guy tackled the problem headfirst by _____.
6. The headline in today's paper is: _____.
7. Although he tried his best, Craig could make no headway against

   _____

8. An example of when Greg acted high-handed is the time when he

   _____

9. We knew Pam was tenderhearted when she _____.
10. I asked Grant for a _____, but he is so tightfisted, he said no.
11. Our teacher was tight-lipped about what would _____.
12. Never trust a person who is underhanded because _____.

ACTIVITY 161 Write Alliterative Sentences

Name: _____

Date: _____

Alliteration is the use of several words together that begin with the same sound.
Example: Barry's brainstorm backfired badly.

For each word, write a short alliterative sentence on another sheet of paper. Use at least three words that begin with the same letter as the compound word.

1. brainstorm
2. bullheaded
3. butterfingers
4. footloose
5. headfirst
6. headline

7. headway
8. high-handed
9. tenderhearted
10. tightfisted
11. tight-lipped
12. underhanded

ACTIVITY 162 Test-Taking

Name: _____

Date: _____

Circle "T" for true or "F" for false.

1. T   F   A **high-handed** person is very bossy.
2. T   F   A person who is **footloose** needs to see a foot doctor.
3. T   F   A person who is **underhanded** is a good tennis player.
4. T   F   A **tightfisted** person does not spend money for unnecessary things.
5. T   F   **Headlines** are wrinkles on someone's head.
6. T   F   If a person is **bullheaded**, he likes to eat vegetables.
7. T   F   Someone who is **tenderhearted** should see a heart specialist.
8. T   F   To be **tight-lipped** means to not say much about something.
9. T   F   To **brainstorm** means to toss ideas around to find a solution.
10. T   F   To do something **headfirst** means to think carefully before acting.
11. T   F   To make **headway** means to make progress.
12. T   F   When a person has **butterfingers**, washing them will help.

Answer Keys

Activity 1 (p. 1)
1. supervisor   2. custodian   3. committee
4. customer   5. coward   6. companion
7. individual   8. tenant   9. relative

Activity 2 (p. 1)
1. *Circle:* individual, people   *Underline:* Abraham Lincoln
2. *Circle:* customer   *Underline:* Amy Johnson
3. *Circle:* companion, trip   *Underline:* Ernie Black
4. *Circle:* audience   *Underline:* Jay Brown, Eun-Jung Kim
5. *Circle:* custodian, school   *Underline:* Joel Jamison
6. *Circle:* relatives   *Underline:* Grandpa Ross, Aunt Marie
7. *Circle:* supervisor, office   *Underline:* Fran Parks
8. *Circle:* coward   *Underline:* Noel Weber
9. *Circle:* committee   *Underline:* Paula White, Ted Green
10. *Circle:* tenants, building   *Underline:* Su Ling, Jean Jensen

Activity 3 (p. 2)
Answers will vary.

Activity 4 (p. 2)
1. b   2. c   3. a   4. b   5. d   6. a
7. b   8. a

Activity 5 (p. 3)
1. e   2. i   3. d   4. f   5. a   6. j
7. b   8. c   9. g   10. h

Activity 6 (p. 3)
In any order 1–6: decrease and increase; exhale and inhale; exterior and interior; frequent and seldom; permanent and temporary; primary and secondary; 7.–10. Answers will vary.

Activity 7: (p. 4)
1. Frequent   2. inhale   3. permanent
4. secondary   5. decrease   6. primary
7. exhale   8. seldom   9. interior
10. temporary

Activity 8: (p. 4)
1. a   2. a   3. b   4. d   5. a   6. c   7. c
8. a   9. b   10. a   11. b   12. b

Activity 9 (p. 5)
1. b   2. f   3. h   4. a   5. j   6. d   7. g
8. c   9. e   10. i

Activity 10 (p. 5)
1. scold   2. gather   3. assemble   4. gaze
5. pretend   6. convince   7. assume   8. recognize
9. despise; complain

Activity 11 (p. 6)
1. assembled   2. complained   3. despised
4. gazed   5. recognized   6. assumed
7. convinced   8. gathered   9. pretended
10. scolded   11. assembled   12. complained
13. convince

Activity 12 (p. 6)
1. c   2. a   3. b   4. d   5. c   6. d   7. d
8. d   9. c   10. a

Activity 13 (p. 7)
1. sleet   2. tornado   3. zephyr   4. hurricane
5. blizzard   6. precipitation   7. humidity   8. climate
9. forecast   10. moisture

Activity 14 (p. 7)
Answers will vary. Possible answers include:
1. cold temperatures and strong winds
2. Weather concerns what is happening now and in the recent past. Climate concerns patterns that can be tracked over long periods of time.
3. Fog or some type of precipitation

4. sustained winds of more than 74 miles per hour
5. Answers could include snow; sleet, hail.
6. Answers will depend on local forecast.
7. high winds, rain, and hail
8. gale, breeze, gust, etc.

Activity 15 (p. 8)
Teacher check.

Activity 16 (p. 8)
1. a   2. c   3. b   4. d   5. a   6. c   7. b
8. a

Activity 17 (p. 9)
1.–10. Answers will vary. Teacher check.
11. factories   12. bays   13. peninsulas
14. meadows

Activity 18 (p. 9)
1. Africa, Antarctica, Asia, Australia, Europe, North America, South America
2. Florida   3. Wisconsin   4. Grand Canyon
5.–10. Answers will vary.

Activity 19 (p. 10)
Rhymes and poems will vary.

Activity 20 (p. 10)
1. F   2. F   3. T   4. F   5. F   6. T
7. T   8. T   9. T   10. F

Activity 21 (p. 11)
1. back / space   2. cloud / burst   3. day / break
4. flood / lights   5. half / way   6. head / light
7. knee / cap   8. screw / driver   9. under / foot
Definitions will vary.

Activity 22 (p. 11)
1. daybreak; <u>daylong</u>   2. headlight; <u>underway</u>
3. halfway; <u>Greenwood</u>; <u>breakfast</u>
4. screwdriver; <u>birdhouse</u>   5. kneecap; <u>cupboard</u>; <u>hallway</u>
6. underfoot; <u>bulldog</u>; <u>housework</u>
7. payday; <u>armchair</u>; <u>houseboat</u>
8. cloudburst; <u>floodwater</u>; <u>underpass</u>

Activity 23 (p. 12)
1. Words and sentences will vary.

Activity 24 (p. 12)
1. T   2. F   3. T   4. F   5. T   6. F   7. T
8. T   9. T   10. T

Activity 25 (p. 13)
Nouns are: bay, bayou, blizzard, canyon, climate, continent, decrease, exterior, hurricane, increase, interior, meadow, peninsula, permanent, precipitation, zephyr
Antonyms are: decrease and increase; exhale and inhale, exterior and interior; frequent and seldom; permanent and temporary; primary and secondary

Activity 26 (p. 13)
Answers will vary.

Activity 27 (p. 14)
Answers will vary. *Some answers include:* backspace; cloudburst; daybreak; halfway; headlights; kneecap; kneepads; overpay; payday; screwball; screwdriver; taillights; underpay; underway

Activity 28 (p. 14)
1. n   2. o   3. g   4. e   5. m   6. i   7. f
8. c   9. l   10. a   11. d   12. j   13. b   14. k
15. h

Activity 29 (p. 15)
1. d   2. j   3. h   4. a   5. i   6. b   7. g
8. e   9. c   10. f

Activity 30 (p. 15)
1. Lent   2.–4. Answers will vary.
5. yeast, flour, water; may include other ingredients
6. gravel
7. Answers will vary: political platform, diving platform
8. Medicines that can be purchased without a doctor's permission

Activity 31 (p. 16)
Answers will vary.

Activity 32 (p. 16)
1. G   2. C   3. E   4. I   5. B   6. A   7. F
8. D   9. H

Activity 33 (p. 17)
Answers will vary. Teacher check.

Activity 34 (p. 17)
Answers will vary. Number 9 would make a good discussion question for a class.

Activity 35 (p. 18)
1. shiver   2. peek   3. erase   4. wander
5. collapse   6. reply   7. wonder   8. depart
9. rescue   10. finish

Activity 36 (p. 18)
1. S   2. S   3. A   4. S   5. S   6. A   7. A
8. A   9. A   10. S   11. S   12. A   13. A   14. S
15. S   16. A   17. S   18. A   19. A   20. S

Activity 37 (p. 19)
1. kindness   2. tired   3. ability
4. recollection   5. trouble   6. chance
7. fear
8. forms an opinion without checking the facts
9. curious
10. a custom that began many, many years ago

Activity 38 (p. 19)
Answers will vary.

Activity 39 (p. 20)
Journal entries will vary.

Activity 40 (p. 20)
1. b   2. d   3. a   4. b   5. c   6. a   7. d
8. c   9. b   10. d

Activity 41 (p. 21)
Definitions will vary. Teacher check.

Activity 42 (p. 21)
1. equip   2. assign   3. employ
4. excite   5. advertise   6. improve
7. advance   8. amend   9. manage
10. accomplish   11. embarrass   12. adjust

Activity 43 (p. 22)
Sentences will vary. Check for correct spelling of past tense.

Activity 44 (p. 22)
1. T   2. T   3. F   4. F   5. F   6. T   7. T
8. F   9. T   10. T   11. T   12. F

Activity 45 (p. 23)
1. e   2. d   3. a   4. l   5. b   6. i   7. c
8. j   9. h   10. f   11. g   12. k

Activity 46 (p. 32)
1. accomplish   2. advance   3. amend
4. embarrass   5. equip   6. improve
7. adjust   8. advertise   9. assign
10. employ   11. excite   12. manage
13.–15.   Sentences will vary. Teacher check.

Activity 47 (p. 24)
Answers will vary.

Activity 48 (p. 24)
1. T   2. T   3. T   4. F   5. F   6. F   7. F
8. T   9. F   10. F   11. T   12. T

Activity 49 (p. 25)
1. modify   2. occupy   3. defend   4. summarize
5. delay   6. fumble   7. amplify   8. accelerate
9. attempt   10. roam
11. makes sound louder; amplify
12. a person who lives in a place; occupy
13. a brief overview of the main points
14. a change

Activity 50 (p. 25)
Sentences will vary. Teacher check.

Activity 51 (p. 26)
1.–4.   Antonyms will vary. Teacher check.
5.–10.   Synonyms will vary. Teacher check.
11.–15.   Sentences will vary.

Activity 52 (p. 26)
1. b   2. c   3. a   4. d   5. a   6. c   7. d
8. b   9. b   10. d

Activity 53 (p. 27)
1.–14.   Antonyms will vary. Teacher check.
15.–28.   Synonyms will vary. Teacher check.

Activity 54 (p. 27)
1. N   2. N   3. V   4. V   5. N   6. N   7. N
8. V   9. N   10. V   11. V   12. N   13. V   14. V
15. N   16. N   17. V   18. N

Activity 55 (p. 28)
1. adjusted   2. equipped   3. improved
4. amended   5. collapsed   6. departed
7. erased   8. finished   9. peeked
10. rescued   11. shivered   12. wandered
13. wondered   14. accomplished   15. advanced

Activity 56 (p. 28)
1. d   2. m   3. k   4. j   5. h   6. b   7. o
8. c   9. e   10. p   11. a   12. g   13. i   14. n
15. q   16. l   17. f

Activity 57 (p. 29)
1. sketch   2. catalog   3. offer   4. crop
5. purchase   6. grasp   7. grasp   8. catalog
9. offer   10. protest   11. experience
12. stall   13. protest   14. deposit   15. crop
16. purchase   17. sketch   18. deposit   19. experience
20. stall

Activity 58 (p. 29)
1. Crop   2. offer   3. grasp   4. sketch
5. experience   6. deposit   7. catalog   8. protest
9. stall   10. stall   11. purchase
12. sketch   13. offer

Activity 59 (p. 30)
Answers will vary.

Activity 60 (p. 30)
1. F   2. F   3. F   4. T   5. F   6. T   7. T
8. T   9. F   10. F   11. T   12. F   13. T   14. F
15. F   16. F

Activity 61 (p. 31)
1. slender   2. essential   3. gigantic
4. circular   5. gorgeous   6. severe
7. delicious   8. awkward   9. generous
10. diagonal

Activity 62 (p. 31)
1. gorgeous   2. delicious   3. gigantic
4. slender   5. diagonal   6. essential
7. generous   8. awkward   9. severe
10. circular

Activity 63 (p. 32)
Answers will vary.

Activity 64 (p. 32)
1. c   2. d   3. a   4. c   5. c   6. b   7. d
8. b   9. d   10. a
Activity 65 (p. 33)
1. possible   2. proper   3. capable
4. appropriate   5. sincere   6. practical
7. inappropriate   8. inequality   9. inflexible
10. incapable   11. impossible   12. impractical
Activity 66 (p. 33)
Answers will vary.
Activity 67 (p. 34)
1. flexible   2. insincere   3. proper
4. inflexible   5. inequality   6. sincere
7. incapable   8. inappropriate 9. possible
10. impractical   11. improper   12. capable
Activity 68 (p. 34)
1. a   2. d   3. b   4. d   5. b   6. b   7. b
8. b   9. c   10. b   11. d   12. d   13. b   14. c
15. d
Activity 69–70 (p. 35)
Answers will vary. Teacher check.
Activity 71 (p. 36)
1. cross over   2. first hand   3. hardship
4. layover   5. overview   6. push over
7. roll over   8. underdog   9. understudy
10. hardware
Activity 72 (p. 36)
1. c   2. b   3. d   4. a   5. b   6. c   7. d
8. c   9. b
Activity 73 (p. 37)
1. disagree   2. unavailable   3. disbelief
4. unbelievable   5. discontinue   6. undesirable
7. dishonest   8. unknown   9. unlimited
10. unnecessary
Activity 74 (p. 37)
1. limited   2. unavailable
3. disagree   4. unbelievable; disbelief
5. known; honest   6. necessary
7. desirable   8. available; discontinue
Activity 75 (p. 38)
Dialogue will vary.
Activity 76 (p. 38)
1. c   2. b   3. c   4. a   5. c   6. b   7. b
8. a   9. c   10. b
Activity 77 (p. 39)
1. l   2. i   3. e   4. b   5. f   6. h   7. d
8. a   9. c   10. k   11. j   12. g
13. Definitions will vary.
Activity 78 (p. 39)
Persons: bachelor; champion; merchant
Places: auditorium; field; museum; cavern
Things: parachute; fragrance
Ideas: conflict; duty; victory
Questions: Answers will vary.
Activity 79 (p. 40)
1. O   2. F   3. O   4. O   5. O   6. O   7. F
8. O   9. F   10. O   11. O   12. O
13.–14. Answers will vary.
Activity 80 (p. 40)
1. d   2. b   3. d   4. d   5. b   6. a   7. a
8. b   9. d

Activity 81 (p. 41)
People: bachelor; champion; customer; merchant; pushover; underdog; understudy
Places: auditorium; cavern; field; museum
Things: catalog; crop; crossover; deposit; fragrance; hardware; parachute; purchase; rollover; sketch; stall
Ideas: belief; conflict; duty; experience; hardship; honesty; honor; offer; overview; protest; talent
Activity 82 (p. 42)
1.–3. Answers will vary.
Activity 83 (p. 42)
Nouns will vary. Teacher check.
Activity 84 (p. 42)
1. victory   2. sketch   3. catalog   4. fragrance
5. capable   6. flexible   7. equality   8. essential
9. delicious   10. severe   11. proper
12. catalog   13. protest   14. sincere   15. conflict
16. protest   17. proper   18. generous   19. awkward
20. experience   21. merchant   22. crop
23. sketch   24. experience   25. stall   26. crop
Activity 85 (p. 43)
1. visual   2. exact   3. regular   4. instant
5. keen   6. former   7. actual   8. natural
Activity 86 (p. 43)
Answers will vary. Teacher check.
Activity 87 (p. 44)
Answers will vary. Teacher check.
Activity 88 (p. 44)
1. b   2. c   3. a   4. d   5. c   6. b   7. c
8. a   9. d   10. b   11. a   12. b
Activity 89 (p. 45)
1. actual   2. annual   3. exact   4. former
5. gradual   6. instant   7. keen   8. natural
Definitions will vary.
Activity 90 (p. 45)
1. exactly; to what extent (how much)
2. Formerly; when   3. gradually; to what extent
4. naturally; how   5. regularly; when
6. Typically; to what extent 7. Usually; when
8. keenly; how   9. visually; to what extent
10. Actually; why   11. annually; when
Activity 91 (p. 46)
Articles will vary.
Activity 92 (p. 46)
1. b   2. a   3. b   4. c   5. d   6. d   7. b
8. c   9. a   10. b   11. d   12. c
Activity 93 (p. 47)
1. a channel built to carry water   2. no   3. Alaska
4. a symbol on a map with points for the directions
5. east and west
6. weather, rain, wind, the cutting down of forests
7. longitude; latitude
8. Hawaii, Alaska, Washington, California, Oregon
Activity 94 (p. 47)
Reports will vary.
Activity 95 (p. 48)
1. O   2. O   3. O   4. F   5. O   6. O   7. O
8. F   9. F   10. F   11. O   12. F   13. O
Activity 96 (p. 48)
1. c   2. b   3. a   4. d   5. b   6. a   7. c
8. d   9. b

Activity 97 (p. 49)
1. to pry something or to use as a lever
2. It is a swimming stroke.   3. a steady jogging pace
4. rough-and-tumble fooling around
5. a person who drops garbage in a public place
6. mischief, usually harmless   7. a bad dream
8. a small cubbyhole, often in a desk
9. a flower   10. a grumpy person

Activity 98 (p. 49)
1. pigeonhole   2. crowbar   3. dog paddle
4. sawhorse   5. snapdragon   6. dogtrot

Activity 99 (p. 50)
1. sourpuss   2. monkeyshines   3. Horseplay
4. Horseradish   5. Snapdragons   6. litterbug
7. sawhorse   8. crowbar   9. dogtrot
10. pigeonhole   11. nightmare   12. dog paddle

Activity 100 (p. 50)
1. b   2. a   3. b   4. b   5. a   6. a   7. b
8. b   9. a   10. a

Activity 101 (p. 51)
1. ambulance   2. automobile   3. aviation
4. cargo   5. carriage   6. marine
7. helicopter   8. motorcycle   9. stagecoach
10. vehicle

Activity 102 (p. 51)
1.–8.   Check answers for reasonableness.

Activity 103 (p. 52)
Land: ambulance; bicycle, train, taxi; go-cart; tractor; truck; motorcycle
Air: airplane; helicopter; blimp; hot-air balloon
Marine: rowboat; ship; canoe; kayak; raft; submarine

Activity 104 (p. 52)
1. b   2. c   3. a   4. a   5. c   6. c   7. c
8. a   9. d   10. b

Activity 105 (p. 53)
1. d   2. f   3. k   4. c   5. i   6. a   7. h
8. l   9. e   10. j   11. g   12. b

Activity 106 (p. 53)
1.–6. Order will vary.
1. ascend and descend   2. borrow and loan
3. export and import   4. external and internal
5. factual and fictional   6. minimum and maximum
7.–10., 13. Answers will vary.   11. ascend
12. internal

Activity 107 (p. 54)
1. borrow   2. descend   3. export
4. external   5. factual   6. fictional
7. import   8. loan   9. maximum
10. minimum

Activity 108 (p. 54)
1. b   2. c   3. a   4. b   5. d   6. b   7. d
8. a   9. b   10. d   11. d   12. a

Activity 109 (p. 55)
Synonyms will vary. Teacher check.

Activity 110 (p. 55)
1. equator   2. lines of latitude   3. lines of longitude
4. compass rose   5. aqueduct   6. stagecoach
7. carriage   8. volcano

Activity 111 (p. 56)
1. d   2. g   3. c   4. a   5. j   6. i   7. b
8. e   9. f   10. h

Activity 112 (p. 56)
1.–10. Nouns will vary.

Activity 113 (p. 57)
Answers will vary.

Activity 114 (p. 57)
1. a   2. b   3. b   4. d   5. c   6. c   7. d
8. b   9. a   10. d

Activity 115 (p. 58)
2. adequate   3. anxious   4. drastic
5. frigid   6. immediate   7. moderate
8. obvious   Definitions will vary. Teacher check.

Activity 116 (p. 58)
1. absolutely   2. adequate   3. anxious
4. adequately   5. drastic   6. frigid
7. immediate   8. immediately   9. obvious
10. Obviously   11. previously   12. absolute
13. anxiously   14. drastically

Activity 117 (p. 59)
Journal entries will vary.

Activity 118 (p. 59)
1. d   2. b   3. b   4. b   5. a   6. d   7. c
8. b   9. c   10. d

Activity 119–120 (p. 60)
Answers will vary.

Activity 121 (p. 61)
1. attract   2. construction   3. construct
4. instruct   5. collect   6. attraction
7. instruction(s)   8. infect   9. infection
10. protection

Activity 122 (p. 61)
1. T   2. F   3. F   4. F   5. T   6. T   7. F
8. T   9. F   10. T   11. T   12. F

Activity 123 (p. 62)
1a. back / up   b. grounds / keeper   c. live / stock
d. over / come   e. over / do   f. over / due
g. over / shoes   h. over / turn   i. stock / room
j. stock / yard   k. turn / over   l. wet / suit
2. Answers will vary.

Activity 124 (p. 62)
Answers will vary.

Activity 125 (p. 63)
1. back up   2. groundskeeper   3. over, come
4. over, do   5. overdue   6. over shoes
7. over, turn   8. livestock   9. stock rooms
10. stockyards   11. turn over

Activity 126 (p. 63)
1. T   2. F   3. F   4. F   5. T   6. F   7. F
8. T   9. F   10. F   11. T   12. T

Activity 127 (p. 64)
1. the study of life   2. plants
3. the study of animals   4. chemicals
5. the study of the earth   6. related to the sun
7. related to the moon   8. related to the stars
9. mathematician   10. historian

Activity 128 (p. 64)
1. biologist   2. botanist   3. geologist
4. scientist   5. zoologist   6. energy from the sun
7.–10. Answers will vary.

Activity 129 (p. 65)
1. Geology   2. stellar   3. solar
4. lunar   5. Zoology; biology   6. zoologist
7. geologist   8. botany   9. botanist
10. chemist   11. historian

Activity 130 (p. 65)
1. T   2. F   3. F   4. F   5. T   6. F   7. T
8. T   9. F   10. F   11. F   12. F   13. T   14. F

85

Activity 131 (p. 66)
Sentences will vary. Teacher check.

Activity 132 (p. 66)
1. penalties   2. discoveries   3. varieties
4. apologies   5. technologies   6. properties
7. quantities   8. deputies   9. deliveries
10. melodies

Activity 133 (p. 67)
Headlines will vary.

Activity 134 (p. 67)
1. a   2. b   3. a   4. b   5. d   6. c   7. b
8. a   9. c   10. d

Activity 135 (p. 68)
Synonyms will vary. Teacher check.

Activity 136 (p. 68)
Sentences will vary. Teacher check.

Activity 137 (p. 69)
Compound words will vary. Some answers include: groundskeeper, overcome, overdo, overdue, overshoes, turnover, suitcase, wetsuit, backyard, backup, stockyard, livestock, upstairs

Activity 138 (p. 69)
1. ADJ   2. V   3. ADV   4. N
5. ADJ   6. N   7. N   8. ADJ
9. N   10. ADJ   11. N   12. N
13. ADJ   14. N   15. N   16. ADV
17. ADJ   18. N   19. N   20. ADV
21. ADJ   22. N   23. N   24. ADV
25. ADJ   26. ADV   27. ADV   28. N
29. V   30. N   31. N   32. N
33. N   34. V   35. N   36. ADV

Activity 139 (p. 70)
1. roadrunner   2. hedgehog   3. turtledove
4. sailfish   5. polecat   6. jellyfish
7. wolfhound   8. sapsucker

Activity 140 (p. 70)
Snakes: cottonmouth, rattlesnake
Mammals: hedgehog, polecat, wolfhound
Birds: roadrunner, sapsucker, turtledove
Insects: silkworm, silverfish
Land animals: cottonmouth, hedgehog, polecat, rattlesnake, roadrunner, sapsucker, silkworm, silverfish, turtledove, wolfhound
Sea animals: jellyfish, sailfish (A cottonmouth is often found in water.)

Activity 141 (p. 71)
Definitions will vary. Share the best ones with the class.

Activity 142 (p. 71)
1. d   2. b   3. a   4. b   5. c   6. d   7. c
8. b   9. c   10. d

Activity 143 (p. 72)
1. l   2. d   3. k   4. g   5. b   6. a   7. j
8. e   9. h   10. f   11. c   12. i

Activity 144 (p. 72)
1. comparison   2. conclusion   3. convention
4. delegation   5. representative
6. denial; provisions   7. production   8. situation

Activity 145 (p. 73)
2. conclude   3. consider   4. convene
5. delegate   6. deny   7. ignore
8. legislate   9. produce   10. provide
11. represent   12. situate
Definitions will vary.

Activity 146 (p. 73)
1. c   2. a   3. c   4. d   5. a   6. c   7. a
8. c   9. d   10. b

Activity 147 (p. 74)
1. prevent   2. contribute   3. combine
4. explain   5. locate   6. refrigerate
7. concentrate   8. detain   9. examine
10. demonstrate   11. compete   12. inform

Activity 148 (p. 74)
1. examine   2. detain   3. explain
4. refrigerate   5. combine   6. concentrate
7. contribute   8. demonstrate or explain
9. inform   10. compete

Activity 149 (p. 75)
E-mails will vary. Teacher check.

Activity 150 (p. 75)
1. S   2. S   3. S   4. A   5. A   6. A   7. A
8. S   9. A   10. A   11. A   12. S   13. S   14. S
15. A   16. S   17. S   18. A   19. S   20. A

Activity 151 (p. 76)
1. i   2. f   3. a   4. g   5. b   6. l   7. k
8. e   9. h   10. d   11. j   12. c

Activity 152 (p. 76)
1. combine   2. concentrate   3. demonstrate
4. examine   5. inform   6. prevent
7. compete   8. contribute   9. detain
10. explain   11. locate   12. refrigerate

Activity 153 (p. 77)
1. information   2. refrigeration   3. location
4. competition   5. detention   6. combination
7. contribution   8. concentration   9. examination
10. demonstration

Activity 154 (p. 77)
1. b   2. b   3. c   4. b   5. a   6. a   7. c
8. a   9. b   10. c   11. a   12. b

Activity 155 (p. 78)
1. capitol   2. capital   3. sympathy   4. liter
5. comma   6. coma   7. litter   8. dessert
9. desert   10. symphony   11. irritate   12. irrigate

Activity 156 (p. 78)
1. irrigate   2. coma   3. capital   4. desert
5. sympathy   6. irritate   7. liter   8. capitol
9. litter   10. comma   11. dessert   12. symphony

Activity 157 (p. 79)
1. F   2. O   3. F   4. O   5. O   6. O   7. F
8. O   9. F   10. F   11. O   12. F

Activity 158 (p. 79)
1. c   2. d   3. a   4. b   5. a   6. c   7. d
8. c   9. a   10. b

Activity 159 (p. 80)
1. d   2. l   3. h   4. e   5. b   6. a   7. i
8. k   9. c   10. g   11. j   12. f

Activity 160 (p. 80)
Answers will vary.

Activity 161 (p. 81)
Sentences will vary.

Activity 162 (p. 81)
1. T   2. F   3. F   4. T   5. F   6. F   7. F
8. T   9. T   10. F   11. T   12. F